HITTING THE HEADLINES!
how to get great publicity

HITTING THE HEADLINES!
how to get great publicity

Iain Pattison

Otter Publications
Chichester, England

© Copyright Otter Publications 1996

First published in 1996 by **Otter Publications**, 5 Mosse Gardens, Fishbourne, Chichester, West Sussex, PO19 3PQ.

No part of this book may be reproduced or transmitted in any form or by any means without permission in writing from the publisher, except by a reviewer who wishes to quote brief passages in connection with a review written for insertion in a magazine, newspaper or broadcast.

British Library Cataloging in Publication Data
A CIP record for this book is available from the British Library.
ISBN 1 899053 05 0

Text design by Angela Hutchings.
Cover design by Jim Wilkie.
All cartoons by Simon Golding.
Printed and bound in Great Britain by Hartnolls Ltd., Bodmin.
Distributed in the UK by Grantham Book Services, Isaac Newton Way, Alma Park Industrial Estate, Grantham, Lincolnshire, NG31 9SD.
The Otter Publications logo is reproduced from original artwork by David Kitt.

TABLE
OF
CONTENTS

INTRODUCTION

PLAYING THE GAME

Many club secretaries and society chairmen believe that there is a media conspiracy against them. Whatever they do they can't get coverage in their local paper or a mention on their local radio station. Reporters just don't want to know.

They point to rival clubs who regularly receive glowing coverage and ask why don't **we** get the same great publicity? Why doesn't anyone write about **us**? They argue that they're the victims of discrimination, claiming that the newspaper is "playing favourites" or "looking after its friends".

It's an understandable reaction - that's how it must look to a casual observer. But the truth is that there are no conspiracies or secret friendships. Editors don't play favourites when it comes to allocating coverage.

If your rivals are getting their name in print while you languish in obscurity, it's down to one thing - they've studied how the media works and how best to exploit its resources. They've learnt the rules of the publicity game.

While you've been waiting for headlines to come to you, they've taken the initiative and made the approaches. They've learnt what a journalist is looking for in a story and done their best to provide him with dazzling quotes and unusual photo opportunities.

Getting great publicity isn't difficult. Anyone can do it. Publicity techniques are simple and easy to learn. So if you're missing out - read on. *HITTING THE HEADLINES!* will explain what your rivals are doing **RIGHT** that you're doing **WRONG**.

Using insider tips on how the media works, who to contact, the best times and methods of approach, making a sales pitch and how to handle press enquiries effectively, this detailed guide shows you how to play the publicity game and win.

Whether you're a businessman wanting to raise the profile of your company, the chairman of a charity wanting to boost your donations, or the secretary of a pressure group fighting to save a woodland from redevelopment you'll find invaluable advice on getting your story into print.

CHAPTER ONE

WHAT IS PUBLICITY?

Publicity means different things to different people. To some it means the circus-like hullabaloo whipped up to draw attention to the opening of a new restaurant or film or the publishing of a famous writer's latest blockbuster.

To others, publicity is seeing a two-line write-up on their Sunday league football team printed in the sports pages of their local freesheet newspaper.

Actually, publicity is all these things and more. It is the coverage that newspapers, magazines, trade journals, radio bulletins and TV programmes give to a multitude of clubs, societies, charities, businesses and sports teams. It is the millions of news stories that tell the world what these organisations and individuals are doing, when they are holding events the public might want to visit and when they need the public's help and support.

Publicity comes in many forms, from the single paragraph news item advertising a jumble sale to the campaign to save an endangered species, but all publicity has a common aim - to attract public attention, win support and spread a message.

1.1 WHY BOTHER WITH PUBLICITY?

The British tend to be suspicious of those who seek publicity. We are renowned for being reserved and modest. We don't shout about our triumphs or bang the drum about our excellence.

Too many people shy away from publicity, thinking it is bragging or showing off. But publicity plays an important role in modern life. Success - especially business success - is judged not by how well you are doing, but by how well you are seen to be doing.

If you don't publicise your achievements, you'll be viewed as a failure. You may not like this, but if rival firms publicise their glories and products, you *must* publicise yours or risk being judged inferior.

The question isn't *Why Bother With Publicity?* but *Can You Dare to Ignore It?*

1.2 DON'T CONFUSE IT WITH HYPE

There is a public misconception that publicity is all about exaggeration, lies, and ego boosting. It's seen as no more than empty media fanfare - a cynical manipulation of people's curiosity. The unsuspecting public are teased and tricked by sharp-suited image men into slavishly buying overpriced products, or visiting lacklustre events.

This is wrong. Publicity isn't about gimmicks, deception or empty hype. It is about passing on accurate, helpful, information to the public - giving them as much knowledge as possible so that they can make reasoned choices.

1.3 BENEFITS OF PUBLICITY

If you're involved with a charity, a sports club, a small business or a pressure group, you'll be amazed by the power of publicity.

It is a dynamic force. It attracts larger crowds to sporting and cultural events, boosts donations to charities, helps draw new members to a host of clubs and societies and lets thousands of potential customers know about the work of small firms.

It boosts public awareness of the work of pressure groups - highlighting social injustices and rallying support for those who seek to put them right. It shines a spotlight on need. It broadens our knowledge of what is going on around us in our towns and cities.

1.4 IT'S EASY TO GET

Many groups who would benefit from media coverage don't get it because they think wrongly that publicity is difficult to get. They assume that their club or charity activities will be of no interest to anyone but their own members. They expect to be ignored by newspapers only concerned in major stories or assume that journalists are only interested in reporting when things go wrong.

The truth is that good publicity is easy to get - far easier than many realise. Newspapers, magazines, radio and TV stations are always willing to give space to publicising the work of local groups - even if it isn't banner headline material. And they like nothing better than carrying *happy* news.

Don't be put off from contacting the media - ironically, many editors wish that they heard from more organisations in their circulation area. The greater variety of news a paper or radio station carries, the more likely it is it increase its audience. If stories about your club sells extra papers, you could be doing the editor a favour!

1.5 AND IT'S FREE

Many people don't realise that publicity is free. The media doesn't charge to put in a news story about you. As long as what you're doing would interest a newspaper's readers, you'll get column inches for nothing. The same goes for broadcast time.

Funnily enough, this free publicity can be more effective than any amount of paid advertising. It has more impact. For one thing, readers don't always look at the adverts - but they tend to read the stories.

More importantly, news stories have more credibility than adverts. Modern readers are cynical about the claims made in adverts - they know someone paid for the words to appear. If the advert says a product is marvellous, they know it's the manufacturer's opinion and treat it with caution.

If, however, a write-up in the editorial columns says the product is marvellous, the reader is more likely to believe it. They know the journalist was impartial and writing what he really thought.

Car manufacturers, film makers and publishers know that one good review by a journalist carries more clout than thousands of pounds of paid advertising.

1.6 TAKE THE INITIATIVE

Publicity doesn't just come along and find you. It doesn't happen by accident - you have to *make* it happen. You have to ensure that journalists are well informed about what you or your group is doing. Someone needs to tell them what's going on - and that person is *you*.

Most news outfits depend on people ringing up or writing in with tip-offs and stories. Although reporters have good contacts and hear about a lot of stories first-hand, they can't possibly know of everything newsworthy that occurs. They need the public to supply them with news.

Don't let your story be one that is missed or overlooked - get cracking and *tell them*!

CHAPTER TWO

PICKING THE RIGHT NEWS MEDIUM

The first question when seeking publicity is: who is most likely to give you media coverage - newspapers, radio, television or trade journals? They all carry varying types of news, presented in different ways, aimed at diverse audiences, and what may excite a newspaper's journalists may fail to spark any interest with TV reporters.

It's up to you to learn what will appeal to each news medium. It's your job to find out what they're all looking for in a story.

Do you know what makes good television or a gripping radio piece? Do you know if your story is interesting enough to attract national coverage or whether it will appeal to only a handful of people in your trade or town? This chapter looks at the news values of each medium - to help you decide where best to target your publicity campaign.

2.1 NEWSPAPERS

Weekly papers

Weekly newspapers are the small fry of the media world. They often have only a handful of journalists on staff - on free newspapers (freesheets) it can be as few as two - and they tend to cover a small geographical area. It may be a town, a cluster of villages or a particular section of a city.

Because they have to find a large number of news stories from a small circulation area, weekly paper editors constantly struggle to fill their pages. This makes weeklies an ideal place to seek coverage.

Not only will an editor welcome you with open arms, but he's likely to give you more column inches than his evening paper counterpart. What might only make a filler in a regional paper will make a whole broadsheet page in a weekly that's short of 'copy'.

Weeklies are useful news outlet but as many have small circulations your story won't reach a large audience. They may only cover an area of a few square miles, so your message is seen in only one locality.

One important point: free newspapers are not highly valued by readers and are often put straight into the bin, unopened.

Evening and regional morning papers

Most provincial towns and cities have an evening paper. Larger cities also have a morning newspaper. In more rural areas, an evening newspaper may cover all or part of a county.

Daily regional papers offer a large audience but you will find it more difficult to get a news item in their columns. You are competing with numerous other groups spread over a large area - all seeking publicity at the same time.

Space is limited in an evening or morning newspaper so if your event or story is only of interest to a small number of readers or affects only one small part of the circulation area it may be relegated to a small mention in an inside page. On a heavy news day, you may fail to make it into print at all.

Stories need more impact than those which appear in a weekly. Routine events like art and craft shows, schools' sports, village carnivals, retirement parties, amateur dramatics productions, visits by the Mayor and individuals winning small competitions are unlikely to attract more than the odd line of coverage.

If you are attempting to get publicity for anything like this you'll have to find a new angle that makes your event stand out from all the others.

Nationals

If interesting a regional paper is difficult, breaking into a national paper's pages can be almost impossible. National stories are often larger than life. They deal with the quirky, the extraordinary and the remarkable - the dead man sent a bill for his own funeral, the tax demand for a penny, the man setting up an ostrich farm in a town centre.

If you think your story is worth national coverage, ask yourself: would this item have people talking in bars the length and breadth of the country? Unless it is unusual enough to excite universal interest, the chances are your story will be rejected.

Many stories appearing in national papers have been sold to them by regional journalists - local freelance 'stringers' or news agencies who've seen the stories printed in their local evening paper and thought that the story had a wider appeal.

If you want national coverage, it's probably worth taking your story first to an evening or morning paper. Once they've printed it, you'll stand more chance of interesting Fleet Street. Alternatively, try taking your story to a local news agency. They'll have the know-how to package your story in just the right way to woo the Mandarins of Wapping.

2.2 RADIO

National

National radio is dominated by the BBC, and its news values tend to reflect those of the 'quality' national papers. Most broadcasts concentrate on world events, international politics, major national stories, parliamentary coverage, and reports on large sporting events.

However, it isn't a totally closed door for the publicity seeker. BBC has regional offices responsible for feeding material into the network (details of BBC regional offices can be found in the Appendix) and Radio 4 has several arts/news/magazine programmes such as Midweek, Woman's Hour and Kaleidoscope which welcome ideas for quirky items.

If you are seeking publicity for a pressure group or campaign you may also think about contacting Talk Radio UK - the independent national radio station, which frequently airs discussions on social problems and national issues.

Local

Local radio offers perhaps the greatest number of publicity opportunities of any broadcast medium. Radio stations, broadcasting up to 24 hours a day, devour material. As well as news bulletins, many stations broadcast 'What's On' features and invite local groups in to the studios to discuss their work and events.

Because the need for material is so pressing, some newsdesks and producers will give coverage to virtually any news story or publicity campaign.

The network is split between BBC stations and independent stations. Independent stations tend to be music-orientated - playing a diet of records interspersed with news bulletins.

BBC stations are speech-orientated, playing fewer records and having more magazine programmes, features, and discussions.

Obviously, BBC stations have more time to give over to interviews so they are a better bet for anyone wanting a 'plug' for their exhibition, carnival, workshop, theatre show or open day. However, BBC stations tend to attract fewer listeners than their independent rivals. So it's always worth seeing if an independent station will give you a mention - maybe have you talking on air for a few moments with a disc jockey.

You may find BBC stations reluctant to help you if they consider your story is no more than a commercial plug for a money-making venture.

2.3 REGIONAL TELEVISION

Television is a visual medium and stories are only used if they can be illustrated with eye-catching moving pictures. Your cheque presentation or petition story may be fine for a newspaper, but may be rejected outright by TV because there's nothing interesting for the cameras to shoot.

It is vital that you think: "how can this story be illustrated?" before approaching a newsdesk. It's the first question you'll be asked.

If your petition demands that a Civil War battle site is saved from a road widening scheme, you'll stand more chance of television coverage if you organise a demonstration at the site or have people in Civil War costumes collecting signatures.

If your disabled group are protesting about the lack of wheelchair ramps in your town centre, one of your members must be prepared to be filmed struggling to get a wheelchair up on to a pavement. Newspapers can describe a problem in words, but television must *show* it in pictures.

Regional television has similar news values to evening newspapers - your story must have impact, relevance and widespread appeal. It costs hundreds of pounds to send a camera crew to cover a story and unless your item will capture the imagination of all of a station's viewers, they won't be interested. Can you say that what you're publicising will fascinate half a million viewers?

Television items are short - some as brief as 15 seconds! Can your story be told simply in a few sentences? Can it be easily understood by a nine-year-old watching the tea time news programme? If not, maybe television isn't the best medium to try.

2.4 TRADE PRESS

If you are trying to attract the attention of people in one particular profession, or those interested in one specific hobby, magazines offer the biggest rewards.

A bewildering assortment of magazines and trade papers exist catering for every job, hobby, trade association, religion, racial group, charity, protest group and interest imaginable. These publications have small circulations, but allow you to target your publicity towards exactly the people you want. They give nationwide coverage.

Because they are catering for a select, knowledgeable audience, trade papers can run stories that are more technical in nature or which deal in great depth with one small facet of a problem affecting only a limited number of people - e.g. how a switch to metric weights forces small corner shops to re-equip with costly new scales.

Many specialist magazines are run from small offices with few staff. Some have part-time editors or amateur editors who are hobby enthusiasts who run the magazine to put them in touch with others who enjoy the same interest.

It's usually easy to gain coverage in such magazines, but you may find yourself asked to write the story yourself and supply your own photographs.

2.5 POINTS TO CONSIDER

- To interest a radio station your story has to be capable of being condensed to under a minute's air time. Listeners have a shorter attention span than TV viewers.
- Don't expect to interest TV in routine events which happen after 7.30 pm. They are too expensive to cover, and any crews on duty will be kept free to film such things as fires, football matches and car crashes.
- Don't expect to interest TV in night-time outdoor events - particularly in winter. These need to be specially lit and most

TV newsrooms will have only one electrician on duty to take care of additional lighting. The same problem affects indoor events where there is poor lighting.

- If you don't have anyone from your group willing to be interviewed on camera, TV news won't be interested.
- The same factor affects newspaper coverage. No paper will carry a story from anonymous 'protesters'. You must have someone willing to have their name printed.
- Local radio newsrooms only have a handful of journalists. After office hours, there may be only one reporter on duty. Don't expect him to come out on a non-urgent job.
- TV crews work to a tight time schedule. If your event is over-running, the crew may have to leave without filming to go on to the next job. Only arrange coverage if you can guarantee the exact time an event will take place.
- No-one expects you to be a master orator, but when being interviewed on television you have to make your point crisply and concisely. You may have only 20 seconds of air time.
- Many radio interviews are conducted live over the telephone. If you haven't got a good telephone manner, put forward a member of your group who does.
- Several BBC radio stations have 'self-operating' mini-studios miles away from the main studio. You may find yourself having to operate the equipment and be interviewed by a disembodied voice over the headphones.
- Don't insist that a reporter interviews everyone in your group. Pick one or two articulate people he can speak to. Even if the reporter humours you and talks to several people, their quotes will end up on the 'cutting room floor.'
- Be organised. Have everyone you need ready in the one place if a reporter is turning up to do a piece on your group. He won't take kindly to being asked to visit several addresses.
- Be prepared to repeat what you're doing several times for a camera crew. They'll need to film the same actions from different angles.

- Reporters are busy people. Don't ask a reporter to call in person if you can give him all the information he needs over the telephone.
- Don't request that a paper send a reporter to cover an event that is only worth a photograph or a short filler paragraph. The reporter will be annoyed and you will risk ruining the chances of future publicity. About 90 per cent of all newspaper stories are covered without the reporter leaving the office.
- Don't 'try it on'. Don't deliberately lie to a news outfit or exaggerate the importance of a story just to guarantee coverage. Editors make powerful enemies.

Remember: just because an event is important to you and your friends, it doesn't mean it's a big news story.

CHAPTER THREE

WHO SHOULD YOU APPROACH?

The thought of getting in touch with a news outfit can be daunting, especially if it's your first time, so it helps if you have a good idea who you should be talking to.

There's nothing worse than ringing up 'blind' relying on the switchboard to put you through to the right extension and then finding that you have to be transferred after explaining your story to the *wrong* person.

You may go into a newspaper front office and find yourself seeing a general news reporter when a sports reporter would be more interested in your story. Target your approach - you owe it to yourself to maximise your chances of success. Before you make any formal approach to a news organisation, try to find out the department you need, the name of someone likely to help and note his correct title and area of responsibility.

3.1 DO YOU NEED THE EDITOR?

The first question is: *do you really need to speak to the top man?* The answer is probably no.

When people ring up they assume they should ask for the editor, but few individuals are put through to him. They are more likely to be put through to the newsdesk.

The editor is a busy man so unless your story is so controversial that it will land the paper in legal problems or involves a fundamental change in editorial policy, he won't need - or want - to speak to you.

In most large media organisations, the editor's job is to look to the future and plan strategies. He will be developing new markets and drawing up editorial policy.

The actual day-to-day gathering and processing of stories will be delegated to his department heads. Of these, the news-editor is probably the most important person for you to talk to.

3.2 WHAT IS A NEWS-EDITOR?

It doesn't matter whether he is called a news-editor, news co-ordinator, head of content, chief reporter, head of input, commissioning editor or any other similar title - his job will always be the same. He is in charge of all news gathering - responsible for ensuring that there are enough stories to fill every page of a newspaper or every minute of a radio or TV broadcast.

He'll know the exact likes and dislikes of his editor - he's been delegated to make news decisions on the editor's behalf - and will choose stories he thinks fit the style, tone and news values set down by the editor. He'll also have an instinctive feel for the type of stories that will intrigue and entertain his readers.

3.3 HE CALLS THE SHOTS

The news-editor is the person who decides if your story is worth using. If he doesn't like it, you won't get coverage. In an average day, he'll be offered dozens of ideas for news items and may say yes to less than half.

He decides whether your story is worth a short two or three paragraph filler or a full-blown story. He'll assess a news item's worth, deciding whether or not to assign a reporter to interviewing you or merely have a copy typist take down a few brief details - perhaps for the paper's *What's On* section.

A news-editor jealously guards the time of his reporters and will only allow a reporter to come out and see you if your story will fill a large amount of space.

3.4 WHEN THE NEWS-EDITOR IS THE EDITOR
On weekly newspapers and trade journals where the editorial staff is small, you may find that there is no journalist with the title of news-editor. In that case, the editor will be working 'hands on', making all the decisions about which stories should be used. Always ring up weekly papers to find out if they have a news-editor or chief reporter who is responsible for making coverage decisions. If not, there's no problem in asking to speak to the editor about your story idea.

3.5 DO YOU REALLY NEED THE NEWSDESK?
Have a moment's thought before contacting a news-editor. Is your story more likely to end up on the sports pages than the general news pages?

Is your publicity idea more likely to make a better in-depth article than a short news story? If so, the features department is probably a better bet - especially if your idea isn't tied-in to a specific date.

Are you really looking for a photographer to cover your event rather than a reporter? If so, the picture editor is the man to speak to. Does the magazine you're targeting have a fashion editor, travel editor or woman's page editor who is more likely to be interested than the newsdesk?

Don't just automatically ask for the news-editor - your idea will be one of hundreds going through the newsdesk. Perhaps dealing with another less-hassled department within editorial will prove more fruitful. The sports editor and features editor have numerous pages to fill as well - and are always on the look-out for material. Also consider specialist correspondents - they can be a good 'doorway' into a newspaper's pages.

3.6 SPECIALIST REPORTERS/ CORRESPONDENTS

It's common for reporters to have special areas of responsibility - as well as their normal general reporting duties. It may be an area of town that they cover (Hillburn Estate reporter) or a topic that they alone write about - health, crime, defence, education, environmental issues, transport, housing, economics, race relations, shopping or industry.

These correspondents will be expected to keep a watching eye on the area or topic they've been assigned and are usually expected to produce a weekly page or regular inserts to broadcast programmes.

It may be that your story - although not of interest to all readers - may fit neatly into the category of news item that a particular 'correspondent' is looking for. Your new assembly line may well interest the industry correspondent or your music festival in Hillburn may be a useful item if the Hillburn page is short of 'copy'.

3.7 EASIER NUT

A correspondent who is struggling to find stories for his page will be an easier nut to crack than the news-editor. He's less likely to say 'no' than the newsdesk.

Some correspondents have total control over what goes into their specialist pages. Others still have to okay content with the news-editor - but they are still worth approaching. If you can convince a specialist reporter that your story is worth covering, it's a good bet that he'll do his best to convince the news-editor that it's a good idea.

This stacks the odds in your favour. The reporter will have more sway over his boss than you have. It's not uncommon for a reporter to talk the news-editor into okaying a story idea that would have been rejected outright if it had gone straight to the newsdesk.

3.8 LOOK FOR NAMES

Look at a few copies of the newspaper you want to approach or watch the TV station you're interested in. Take a note of the names of the reporters - particularly those with relevant specialist 'portfolios'.

Contact the reporter who covers the subject or geographical area you are interested in. Alternatively, see what type of stories certain reporters cover - if a journalist has written about a similar event to yours, he may be worth trying directly.

If you admire the way a particular journalist writes and feel comfortable with him writing about you, ask for him by name.

Having a named person to ask for rather than merely asking for the newsdesk, does give you a head start over others seeking publicity. Every advantage counts.

3.9 TITLES MATTER

Journalists are very touchy about their names and titles being correct. If you write to Doug Hughes, calling him deputy sports editor, when his name is Derek Hughes and he is news-editor, he *will* be displeased.

It's unlikely he'd reject your story over this blunder, but it won't do your chances any good. When you're seeking publicity you rely on the goodwill and patronage of journalists. Don't antagonise them.

Always make sure that you know the name of the news-editor or department head you need. If you are contacting several different news-outlets, do your homework - research them, using a media guide.

3.10 MEDIA GUIDES

There are numerous reference books guides on the market giving detailed listings of radio and TV stations, newspapers, magazines, trade journals and news agencies - including editor's names, news-editor's names, phone numbers, addresses and other useful background information. Always consult a guide if you are planning a large publicity campaign. It'll help you decide which media outlets to approach depending on the geographical area you want to target, the type of readership you want to interest or the subject you want to promote.

3.11 ALWAYS DOUBLE CHECK

A guide will tell you the name of the person you should be approaching and his title or area of responsibility - but don't view the guide as infallible. Always ring up the paper's switchboard to check that the information is correct before speaking to the person you want or addressing a letter to them.

Guides are published annually and it's impossible for a comprehensive listing - no matter how good - to reflect staff changes that occur between editions. It's as impossible as keeping an electoral register up to date, with people constantly moving house.

3.12 SHOULD YOU BUY A GUIDE?

If you think you'll be ringing up newsdesks on a regular basis, a guide is invaluable and is definitely worth buying. If, however, you're seeking only occasional publicity or only intend to deal with your local paper or radio station, then you'd be better to visit a reference library. Most have copies of at least one media guide - most have Willings Press Guide. This hefty two-volume guide is published by Reed Information Services and offers information on all media outlets across the globe.

For details contact Reed Information Services, Windsor Court, East Grinstead House, East Grinstead RH19 1XA. Tel: 01342 32672

3.14 RECOMMENDED GUIDES

If you are thinking of buying a guide, there are three inexpensive books I can recommend:

THE WRITER'S HANDBOOK, published by Macmillan at £12.99.
THE WRITERS' AND ARTISTS' YEARBOOK, published by A & C Black at £10.99.
THE GUARDIAN MEDIA GUIDE, published by Fourth Estate at £9.99.

Both The Writer's Handbook and The Writers' and Artists' Yearbook are available from High Street bookshops. If you have difficulty obtaining the Guardian Media Guide, write to Fourth Estate Ltd., 6 Salem Road, London W2 4BU. Tel: 0171 727 8993

Addressing news releases and letters to the right person is crucial - every week newsroom receive mountains of wrongly addressed post or mail addressed to staff who left years before. These items often end up in the bin!

CHAPTER FOUR

MAKING CONTACT

You know which newspaper, TV or radio station you want to approach and have found out which news-editor, reporter or specialist writer you need to speak to. The next question is how do you make that initial contact - should you ring, fax, write a letter or go into the front office?

Although many people wouldn't realise it, how you make that first approach can determine whether or not your story makes it into print or goes 'on air'. This chapter looks at the pros and cons of the various methods you may choose. See which style fits in best with your personality, resources and available time.

4.1 ADVANTAGES OF TURNING UP IN PERSON
Personal touch
It's easy to tell someone 'no' over the telephone, or by letter, but it's far harder to let them down face to face. So if you have the opportunity to see a reporter, take it. When you become a 'real'

person and not just a vague, disconnected, voice or a name on a piece of paper, the reporter is more likely to develop a rapport with you.

Personality hooks
If you are out-going and relate well to people then this is by far the most effective way to approach a news outfit. A friendly handshake, a chatty manner and a welcoming smile work well on reporters. They spend so much of their working lives dealing with hostile, frowning, interviewees that a happy face and a polite word make a refreshing change.

Time to relax
With a peak time phone call, you are hurried; always under pressure. The busy reporter, more experienced at phone interviews than you, is likely to dictate the pace and direction of the conversation. You can put the phone down feeling you've been rushed through some uncaring, impersonal, 'sausage processor'.

Visiting a newspaper office gives you the opportunity to tell your story in a more relaxed way. A phone soon becomes heavy to hold, and a reporter always has the hassle of holding the receiver with one hand while writing down notes with the other. It's not surprising he wants to get you off the line as briskly as possible.

Avoiding mistakes
Sometimes, unfortunately, mistakes occur when reporters take notes over the phone. They may mishear you or misunderstand what you're explaining. If the newsroom is busy a reporter may be trying to listen to you over a racket.

If you are there, you're much more likely to get a reporter's undivided attention and he's more likely to listen carefully to what you're telling him. Many newspaper offices have interview rooms or special quiet reception areas.

While being interviewed, you'll be able to tell from the reporter's facial expression, body language and attitude whether or not he is following exactly what you are explaining. If he appears puzzled you can amplify what you're talking about, perhaps explaining it in a different way.

Visual back-up
If the story you're trying to interest a reporter in requires a number of diagrams, photographs, artists' sketches and maps - maybe the site of your new sports stadium or factory - you can bring them along and point out items of interest. Many seemingly complicated stories are easy to explain with the aid of a sketch plan or photo. Some 'legal problem' tales only make sense when the reporter has access to reams of correspondence.

Safeguarding valuable items
Naturally, you may feel reluctant to trust valuable pictures, legal documents or important sketch plans to the post.

If you bring in such items personally, you can vouch for the fact that they were handed over intact. No one can claim that the photograph was mangled in the mail.

Reporters are more likely to take care of an item if they receive it in pristine condition and can tell that you are concerned for its safety.

Many newspapers will copy old photographs - basically taking a picture of a picture - and can do this while you wait. Not only does this give you peace of mind that nothing terrible will happen to the original, but gives the paper a valuable picture to add to its photographic library.

Most editorial offices have photocopiers, so important documents can be copied - allowing you to keep the originals safe.

4.2 DISADVANTAGES
Being overawed
If you are easily intimidated by large, busy offices then it's probably better to contact a news organisation by letter or phone. Even the relative calm of a newspaper reception area

can become a frantic buzz of activity as motorbike couriers deliver and collect packages, customers come in to place classified ads, readers order photo reprints and others, like yourself, come in to speak to reporters.

'Stage fright' can affect anyone - no matter how used they are to office noise and confusion. Even experienced journalists admit to being intimidated when they go into the front offices of ITN's London headquarters.

There's just something about the milling bodies, towering glass floors, the wide expanses of chrome and tiles that makes them feel lost and insignificant.

Bad impression

When you go into a newspaper, everything about your appearance and mannerisms is on display. Reporters will naturally make judgments about you based on how you look and act.

If you are an immaculately turned out, supermodel with no annoying habits then this won't be a problem. But if, like most people, you've just got soaked in the rain, had a child dribble ice-cream over your shoes and become flustered and angry trying to find a parking space, the chances are you won't create the good impression you intended.

This isn't just vanity - looks count. They add to the aura of professionalism. That's why national pressure groups always make sure their spokesmen are well groomed.

Pot luck

Unless you've rung up to make an appointment with a particular journalist, it's likely you'll be seen by whichever reporter happens to be free at the time.

Although the reporter who comes downstairs to talk to you will try to help, you may find that you need to speak to a specialist writer. For example, if you are launching a bottle bank or reclaiming woodland, the paper's environment reporter may wish to speak to you. You can then find yourself having to explain your story a second time - annoying if you've already spent twenty minutes outlining the details.

Worse still, the specialist you need to speak to may be out of the office or tied up with another interview. You may have to wait ages until he becomes free or have to come back on another occasion. To prevent this happening to you, it's a good idea to ring up first and make an appointment to come in on a specific day.

4.3 ADVANTAGES OF RINGING UP

Topicality
Newspaper stories are like bread - fresh today but stale tomorrow. News is a perishable commodity. If your story will be out of date or overtaken by events in a few days, then you can't afford to wait. Get dialling.

Saving time
It would be maddening to go to the trouble and expense of travelling to a newspaper office only to find out that the reporter who sees you doesn't think your story is worth printing. Even at daytime rates, a phone call is usually cheaper than petrol or bus fares. Sound out a newsdesk over the phone.

Anonymity
Although a reporter may be unwilling - for an ordinary, routine story - to deal with someone who won't give his name or any other details, he will probably follow-up a hard news tip-off you give him 'anonymously'.

If you are whistle-blowing on an unscrupulous employer, highlighting an injustice or can't afford to be implicated in a news story for fear of intimidation or reprisals, the phone protects your identity.

Before you ring, make sure that your call isn't being monitored or recorded by a switchboard at your location. Also 'de-activate' the last number re-dial device on the phone and ensure that the reporter cannot find out your number by dialling 1471 after you've rung.

4.4 DISADVANTAGES

Busy lines

Some newspaper offices are notoriously busy - receiving hundreds of phone calls an hour. At frantic times - coming up to editorial deadlines and the cut-off point for placing classified ads - you may find the switchboard jammed.

Then, you face the problem of trying to ensure you are put through to the right person. This is particularly difficult if you don't know whether the announcement of your football club's new star signing is a news story (dealt with by the newsdesk) or a sports story (dealt with by the sports editor). The operator will be keen to put you through to an extension so that she can get on with handling the dozens of other calls. She won't have the time to advise you.

If you end up speaking to the wrong person, he may not be able to help or be able to transfer your call.

Sounding silly

Having a good, crisp phone manner is essential. Unless you are confident and know exactly what you are doing it is easy to become flustered and sound amateurish. If you don't have all the facts at your fingertips, you run the risk of being asked something you can't answer, going away to find out the information and having to ring up a second time.

Apart from the hassle of going through the busy switchboard again and trying to get put back on to the same reporter, you will have given the impression that you are dotty and disorganised and possibly not worth the reporter's time.

Talking to the wrong person

If the reporter you need is out of the office, your call will be handled by whoever happens to hear the phone ringing. Even if he is prepared to sit down and listen to you, all he'll do is write a note for the person you'd rung. He may, unhelpfully to you, add something to the message like: *"It doesn't sound like much of a story to me!"*

Wrong message
Apart from the waste of your time and phone bill speaking to someone who can't help you, there's a chance that in the confusion of a busy newsroom he'll pass on an inaccurate or incomplete message. The message, scribbled on a corner of scrap-paper may even get lost.

Hanging on the phone
Once you've rung up and been told that John Williams isn't in but he'll ring you back as soon as he returns, you've effectively chained yourself to the phone - waiting for it to ring. If John Williams is working on several stories at once, he may not get back to you for hours; maybe not even until the next day.

Getting the brush-off
If you ring and are told: *"Sorry, that reporter is out on an interview at the moment,"* do you know that he really *is* out of the office or merely signalling to a colleague to cover for him because he hates dealing with you?

4.5 ADVANTAGES OF WRITING IN
Cheap and easy
Dropping a quick note to a paper doesn't have to take long - especially if all you're seeking is a simple two paragraph mention for a coffee morning or a change in MP's surgery times. All it takes is a few minutes and the price of a stamp.

Time to gather your thoughts
If you don't think well 'on your feet' and want time to choose the right words, then a letter is ideal. It gives you the chance to check over the facts you're putting down, making sure there's nothing missed out. Even experienced press officers forget important points when a reporter's questions take them off the subject.

Chance to liaise
If members of your club or society are worried about what the newspaper might publish, it gives all interested people the

opportunity to agree a set of words. Everyone sees exactly what information is being given out.

4.6 DISADVANTAGES

Log-jam

News organisations are inundated with mountains of mail - it arrives every day by the sack load. A newsdesk can spend the first hour in the day just opening letters and press releases.

Your letter will be just one in dozens, if not hundreds, to arrive on a news-editor's desk. He hasn't got the time to give detailed consideration to every piece of mail - especially if it is badly written and doesn't make the point in the opening sentences. Your letter could be examined and discarded in less than 30 seconds.

Bad impression

Bearing in mind how little time the news-editor will look at your letter, it isn't likely to capture his interest if it is poorly typed, full of spelling mistakes and tatty looking. It will compare very badly to the slickly produced, beautifully printed, handouts produced by national companies which will rival you for his attention. If your letter is handwritten, with a barely legible scribble, it is likely to fail.

Wrong person

What if your letter ends up on the wrong desk? It does happen, especially when you haven't done your homework and haven't found out the name and title of the reporter you should be contacting.

Most of the mail will arrive at the office addressed to *The Editor*. It will be sorted into rough bundles for the relevant editorial departments, but if your letter goes to the sports desk when it should really have gone to the newsdesk there's no guarantee that it will be redirected.

4.7 FAXING

Only use a fax if you have a 'breaking' story that will go out of date if it isn't printed immediately. If you fax details of an event happening a month away, you may antagonise the newdesk. While you were unnecessarily faxing your story, you may have been preventing an urgent message from getting through.

Faxing isn't totally reliable. Faxes can arrive smudged and difficult to read. They can arrive with pages missing. If the fax machine runs out of paper they may not arrive at all.

It's common for the top sheet of a fax to become separated from the rest of the pages, making it impossible to know who the fax was meant for. Pages of your fax can become muddled up with pages from other faxes.

Smaller news outlets may not have a fax or it may be situated in the managing director's office rather than the newsroom. It may take ages before anyone thinks to pass on the message.

The rule of thumb is: don't fax unless you are asked to.

4.8 E-MAIL

It may well be that in the future electronic mail - sending messages from computer to computer - will become the most common way for people to contact the media. Currently, however, news outfits tend to only use their Internet 'address' to receive reader's letters and other short items. It is still more reliable to use the post or phone to contact a newsdesk.

Remember: no matter how you approach a newsdesk, make sure you have all the necessary information at your fingertips. It's your responsibility to be as professional as possible. Don't waste anyone's valuable time.

CHAPTER FIVE

THE SALES PITCH

Having made contact it's vital to hook the interest of the news-editor. Your news item must excite. You must sell him on the story.

You won't get coverage just because you ask or feel you deserve it - you need to have a sales pitch. You must convince a jaded journalist that you've got just the story to fascinate his readers. You must ooze enthusiasm. You must show that you've thought about the story and have identified the elements that will hold an audience.

A news-editor will be looking for a fresh, lively tale or at least a new, unusual, slant on a familiar subject. Demonstrate that you can deliver the goods. Amaze him!

5.1 FIND THE ANGLE

Look at your story through a journalist's expert eyes. Think what is unusual, quirky or amazing about your event or new product.

Is it the biggest, smallest, loudest, tallest, most expensive, weirdest? Is it a *first*? Is it going to make its way into the record books? Does it feature something bizarre or unexpected - like Grannies roller-skating for charity or supermarket staff dressing up in outlandish costumes?

What is different about your event that will make people talk about it? What is its unique characteristic - *that* will be your angle.

5.2 GET YOUR STORY NOTICED

An angle doesn't have to be earth-shatteringly original or momentous; nor silly or outrageous - it just has to make your story stand out from the crowd.

You may be the principal of an adult education department and want to publicise the 500 varying evening classes you are running through the winter. You approach your local paper but the news-editor thinks evening classes are boring and doesn't want to give you more than a couple of paragraphs of space. What do you do?

Simple. Look through your syllabus and select the classes that are unusual or unconventional and publicise those. Beginners' French may not capture anyone's imagination but The Secrets of the Pharaohs, Famous Hauntings, Build Your Own River Raft and Learn Japanese in 10 Weeks are much more likely to pique the interest of any newsman.

5.3 DON'T BE DOWNBEAT

The marketing world knows that how you package an item is as important as the content. The same is true of news stories. Selecting a good angle is a big help, but if you do little to brighten up your news item, it may not grab a reporter's attention. No-one will want to publicise a boring event.

Be lively - there are no prizes for being dull. You don't need to resort to lies, exaggerations or hype - just make sure you aren't being deadpan or matter-of-fact.

We all know people who can make a single-handed trek across the desert sound as dull as a trip to the dry cleaners and others who can make buying a pair of shoes sound like an adventure.

Entertaining stories stand more chance of being printed. So don't give your lecture a ponderous title like: *'An Examination Of The Possibilities Of The Existence Of Ghosts'* when *'Is Your House Haunted?'* is shorter, punchier and more attention grabbing!

5.4 THINK PICTURES

Even if your story doesn't depend upon illustrations, having sketches, photographs and plans will help to whet the reporter's appetite. If you have an impressive bundle of plans, the story will appear important.

Old sepia photographs are great for capturing the attention of readers, especially elderly readers. So if you are trying to interest your local paper in a story on your class reunion, try showing the reporter the old class picture. That photo may just tickle his interest.

Newspapers always want good picture ideas so stress any photographic opportunities when you make your 'pitch'.

5.5 FOLLOW-UPS

If you've successfully sold a news-editor on your story, don't be content to have just one mention. Always think about possible follow-up stories.

If the newspaper sent along a reporter to cover the launching of your church roof repair appeal, why not invite him back after a year to do an up-date? Readers will be curious to see how your fund-raising has got on and the resulting story will probably bring in a second round of donations.

You don't have to wait for the year - if the appeal reached its target after only a few months, why not get the paper to take a picture of the work being carried out on the roof?

If the paper did a preview story on you taking part in the London Marathon to raise cash for your favourite charity, why not invite them back a couple of months later to photograph you handing over the cash?

Don't wait to be asked. If you think your story is worth an update, contact the news-editor and suggest it. Often he'll be delighted to give you the coverage. The first story will be on file in the cuttings library and a reporter will be able to do the follow-up easily - using the original for reference.

It's always easier to do updates on existing stories, than to find fresh untold stories. And switched-on charities, clubs and businesses know this and exploit it.

5.6 THINK MULTI-MEDIA

Look to maximise the amount of coverage you get from each story. Think how many different news outlets you can approach with the story. Are you only thinking about newspapers when trade journals and local radio could be interested as well? Is there a television angle? Be greedy. Try to get your story featured in as many news outlets as possible.

5.7 PLAY NEWSDESKS OFF AGAINST EACH OTHER

News outfits are terrified of being scooped by their rivals, and tend to slavishly follow each other's lead. If one news-editor agrees to print a story on you or your group, you can mention this fact to news-editors on rival publications. The chances are they'll be keen not to miss out and will also offer coverage.

It can be particularly effective to tell an evening paper news-editor that the local TV station has already shown an interest. He won't want his editor seeing the item on the teatime news programme and demanding to know: *"Why didn't we have that story?"*

Even if there is no deep rivalry between news-editors, the fact that one journalist thinks your story is worth printing normally convinces the others that you're worth interviewing.

If you're uncomfortable with the idea of playing people off against each other, why not offer your story **exclusively** to one newsdesk? The thought of having a story all to himself may help to convince a news-editor to print it.

5.8 MULTIPLE ANGLES

Think how many different angles you can manufacture. If you're organising a steam rally, have you considered how many different stories the event might generate?

You may be used to putting out press releases giving details of rally activities and the numbers of exhibitors and visitors expected. But would you look beyond that for other stories, stories that might guarantee extra coverage on the second and third day of the rally?

Do you have a colourful, eccentric character who'd be great to interview on television? Is there an exhibitor who rebuilt his steam engine from a pile of scrap metal? Is one of your exhibits an unusual traction engine rarely seen by the public? All of these are stories in their own right.

5.9 RE-PACKAGING

You may have a story on your hands that can be re-angled to appeal to numerous news outlets. By re-packaging it, to stress different news points, you may be able to interest journalists in a wide range of publications, across the country.

Let's say that the steam engine rebuilt from scratch is the handiwork of a bank manager from Stapleford. He found the rusting remains of the engine in a barn in Dunston and rebuilt it, helped by a firm in Wirtham who cast special ironwork for him.

Obviously the story will interest the media in Stapleford - that's where the bank manager lives. *Stapleford Man Restores Traction Engine.*

But there is also a strong Dunston link - a pile of scrap metal found in a Dunston barn has been lovingly rescued and restored. That will appeal to journalists in that area. *Dunston Traction Engine Restored.*

Papers in Wirtham will be attracted by the fact that a local firm manufactured its replacement. *Wirtham Firm Helps Traction Engine Rescue.*

Hobbyist magazines may be interested in the story of the years of hard work that went into rebuilding the engine. National newspapers and magazines might use the nostalgia angle. *Historic Engine Returns From The Dead.*

See how all these stories have exploded from one basic idea? Astute freelance writers can re-package material to sell to 20 different outlets. As someone seeking as much publicity as possible you should think the same way - where else could this story be printed or broadcast?

5.10 THREE BITES AT THE CHERRY

Even modest events can offer numerous publicity opportunities. Always think of having three bites at the cherry - a preview story, coverage of the event as it happens and a follow-up story some time after.

For example, you contact your newspaper a few weeks before the village carnival you're organising to arrange a story plugging the event. You arrange for a photographer to come out on the day and give the news-desk your phone number so that a reporter can ring up to find out how the event went. His story will accompany the picture.

A fortnight later you send in a short press release saying how much money was raised, and thanking everyone who helped make the carnival such a success.

CHAPTER SIX

WRITING EFFECTIVE
PRESS RELEASES

Don't worry if you aren't a natural salesmen and can become tongue-tied or nervous. Simply make your sales pitch on paper. Send in a press release setting out the bare bones of your story, but including enough enticing snippets that you'll excite the news-editor's curiosity. Three or four short paragraphs of lively facts can do the trick.

The news-editor will be able to see at a glance if your story interests him. If he thinks it is worth only a filler, the information on your handout will probably be enough. If he's interested in a larger story, the press release will be given to a reporter to follow up.

6.1 GOOD COMPANY
Your press release will be in good company. At least half of all the mail received in an editorial department is press releases.

Large companies regularly send out handouts to alert newsdesks to new products, factory openings, large export orders and the promotion of senior staff. Shops use them to publicise 'half-price sales', and fashion chains regularly send out press releases detailing new season's clothes - complete with photographs of models wearing the latest looks. Even bus companies use them to let journalists know when routes are being changed or fares increased.

6.2 DON'T GO OVER THE TOP

Before sending in a press release, ask yourself: *is my story really important enough to warrant going to the trouble of preparing a detailed handout?* A newsdesk will welcome ten paragraphs from a local firm that has just taken over a rival company following a bitter boardroom battle, but will be bemused by a similar number of paragraphs from an individual who has won fourth prize in his neighbourhood art club's Autumn painting competition.

Keep a sense of proportion. Just because something is important to you doesn't mean it will be important to a newspaper. Always think how your press release will be viewed by a news-editor. Don't make him laugh at you 'going over the top!'

6. 3 LABEL IT CLEARLY

The first thing to do when preparing a news handout is to put the words **Press Release** at the top of the page in a large, bold type. This ensures that, when opened, your handout will go directly to the editorial department and won't accidentally end up in the advertising or accounts departments at the newspaper.

If you are sending the handout to a TV station it may be better to substitute the words **News Release** as some television journalists don't like to be described as members of 'The Press'.

6.4 HEADLINE

Next, put a lively heading near the top of the page, just under the words *Press Release*, which will grab the reader's attention. As well as catching the news-editor's eye, the headline should be a single sentence summary of the press release. e.g. Sommerton Man Scoops £1,000 First Prize in National Crossword Competition or Sommerton Bakery Firm Opens £12-million Factory Extension. This line allows a busy newsdesk to see at a glance if your handout is worth following up for a story.

It is unlikely that your headline will make it into print. It probably won't fit the space allocated and the sub-editors will prefer to put their headline on to the finished story. But you will have helped the news-editor to visualise your item as a story.

6.5 PUNCHY INTRODUCTION

Remember that your first sentence is the most important, so make sure you have a strong opening. It must be arresting, must introduce the story clearly and must lead naturally on to the main body of the text. In journalism there isn't the time or the space to tell a story in chronological order - there's no time for a gradual build-up - so get to the important facts first. Summarise the bare bones of the story in 35 words or less.

6.6 THE MAIN TEXT

Once you've got the reader's attention you can then go on to fill in the wider background details - to put flesh on the skeleton. Your sentences and paragraphs can become a bit longer. Sub-editors often cut stories from the bottom - deleting the final paragraphs first - so make sure all major facts are high up in the text. A press release is *not* the place for a sting-in-the-tail ending!

6.7 THE 5 Ws

Make sure that you answer all the *Who? Where? Why? When? What?* questions. These are known in journalism as the 5Ws. They are usually accompanied by a sixth question - *How?* If you don't answer all the 'W' questions, it's likely that you've missed out an important fact and risk leaving the reader baffled.

6.8 KEEP IT TIGHT

Some news-editors won't read past the first few paragraphs of a press release so keep your text as short and simple as possible. One side of A4 is ideal. Don't ramble, don't repeat yourself and don't include unnecessary detail.

6.9 KEEP IT SIMPLE

A press release should be a collection of straight-forward statements, putting over information in the most direct way possible. The facts are all that counts - not your writing style.

Don't try to show off or try to impress. No amount of fancy phrases will interest a news-editor in a lacklustre story. Stick to a simple sentence structure - with one important fact per sentence - and keep your paragraphs short.

6.10 AVOID CLICHÉS

Always use a simple, clear, concise vocabulary. Don't be obscure and don't use technical expressions, jargon or hackneyed old phrases. A press release should make sense to anyone who reads it - whether they are involved in your profession or not. Make sure you have explained everything fully. Never assume that the journalist will share your level of background knowledge or expertise.

6.11 DON'T USE HYPE

Be lively and intriguing but don't deliberately miss out vital information just to create suspense. News-editors are far too experienced to be taken in by that ploy and you'll annoy the poor reporter who has to waste time chasing up the facts you've hidden. Don't exaggerate or mislead. You'll be found out quickly, as soon as the reporter starts to check through your facts - and you'll run the risk of being permanently blacklisted by the newsdesk that you've tried to con. Never let your desire to see one story in print make you alienate good contacts and ruin future publicity chances. Journalists who've been 'mucked about' have long memories.

6.12 NAMECHECK

Before sending in a press release always make sure you've included your name and address and phone number on the bottom. Many people forget to do this. There's no point interesting a reporter in a story if he doesn't know who to speak to or how to contact you.

Include your extension number, if you have one, and specify times that the reporter will be likely to get hold of you. It's best to give both a daytime number and an evening number.

6.13 PRESENTATION IS VITAL

It's likely that your press release will land on the news-editor's desk at the same time as dozens of others, so you owe it to yourself to make sure your handout is neat, well laid out and easy to read. While no-one expects your press release to be as jazzy as those from large companies and public relations outfits, you don't want your effort to look shabby or amateurish by comparison.

Choose a good paper

Use a good quality paper - A4, 80 gms, white photocopier paper is ideal. It is widely available from stationery shops and is comparatively inexpensive. Don't feel you have to splash out on brightly coloured papers. While a pastel tone might help your press release stand out from the others, a garish dayglow yellow will probably make the news-editor feel ill!

Don't worry, either, about going to the expense of getting special letterheads printed. News-editors are notoriously difficult to impress and a fancy typeface and logo won't win him over if he thinks your story is boring.

Set out the letter neatly

Leave a wide margin on both sides of the page and start several lines down from the top. Also leave a few lines of white space at the bottom of the page. The effect should be that the text looks as if it is surrounded by a white frame.

Double space your text and indent each new paragraph.

Start the new paragraph about six characters (2 cms) in from the left-hand edge of the type. Alternatively, if you don't want to bother with indents, leave a line of white space between paragraphs.

Keep your paragraphs short - maybe only two sentences to a paragraph - and keep your sentences short. Aim to have no more than 35 words per sentence. As well as making your letter more visually appealing, it will help you to stick to the point.

Don't make your typing cramped

Pick a typeface that is large, wide and easy to read. Don't select one where the letters are so small and cramped that the lines look grey. Remember, if a news-editor has any difficulty at all in reading your press release, he'll junk it and switch to something else.

Make sure the typeface on your letter is at least 12pt. If the typing still looks cramped, increase the point size to 14pt. You should be aiming to get about ten words to the line.

Don't use italics, underlining, shaded backgrounds, outline typefaces or any other typographical device just because your word processor or personal computer can do it. Concentrate on being neat - not flashy. A press release isn't the place for layout gimmicks.

6.14 EMBARGOES

Now there may be a good reason for placing an embargo on the news contained in your handout - restricting its publication until a specified date and time. If you are contacting news media across the country, you may need to distribute press releases days before you wish your story to 'go public'.

You may be afraid of giving away commercially sensitive information to a rival firm or not want to cause a panic by having an announcement go out before you have had time to brief your colleagues. The sports star you are signing may not yet have put his signature to the contract or the lucky winner of an award may not yet himself know he's been nominated. It may even be that you want a co-ordinated launch for a campaign or awareness week and need all news media to release the story simultaneously.

In such cases, most news organisations would recognise the wisdom of an embargo and would respect your wishes. However, it is a gentleman's agreement and you can't guarantee that *all* media outfits will abide by the restriction. If a newspaper thinks it can steal a march on its rivals by breaking the embargo and publishing the story 'exclusively', it may disregard your wishes entirely. You have no control over the editor and no matter how annoying or damaging this 'betrayal' is you have no legal recourse against the offending paper.

> **One important point**: embargoes should only be used when *absolutely* necessary. Don't embargo your press release just to give it an air of excitement and suspense.

Also, don't make yourself look stupid by embargoing a trivial news item like the announcement of the date of your amateur dramatic society's next production.

6.15 WORD FOR WORD
Many radio stations and newspapers are run with small numbers of journalists, and news-editors look for any short-cuts they can find. If you are confident of the newsworthiness of your tale, you may think it worth sending in a longer handout - maybe as much as ten (shortish) paragraphs - setting out your story in full. If it is well-written, well-angled and contains all the relevant facts and quotes, the news-editor may put the submitted story straight over to the sub-editors for processing.

The press release may even go into the newspaper word for word as you wrote it. This happens frequently on weekly newspapers which have few reporters and acres of space to fill.

6.16 I WROTE THAT!
It's not unusual for a press officer to submit a press release, have it go into print unaltered and see it appear with a reporter's

byline credit on it - just because the reporter typed it into the office computer system! If this happens to you, don't moan about someone else getting the credit for your work - just take delight in getting your message into print without it being distorted or watered down.

6.17 THE GOOD, THE BAD AND THE UGLY

So what does a good press release look like? And what are the pitfalls to avoid? The best way to answer these questions is to look at examples of typical press releases that arrive daily in a newsroom.

The first is a good, eye-catching release, packed with useful information - guaranteed to intrigue a news-editor. The second is a comprehensive but dull press statement, which does the job but hardly excites. And the third is a jargon-filled business handout which would take a team of Government code breakers to decipher. The person who sent it in deserves to be shot!

Top of the Class

Any news-editor would be delighted to receive a press release like Example 1 - especially if he needed a few paragraphs to fill a hole on the business page. It can be put straight into the paper with only the lightest of re-writes.

It takes a reasonably dull subject - details on a phoneline to help people who lose their credit cards over the Christmas period - and makes it come alive. By using a little thought, and a few anecdotes, this news release has been given the human touch. Even readers who hate credit cards will want to find out about the silly things people ring up to ask the helpline.

All the necessary information is already there - including an amusing quote. But a contact name and number is included - just in case the newsdesk want to turn this quirky item into a full-blown story. Credi-card's PR department know how to get good publicity for free.

Press Release Example 1 : The Good

CREDI-CARD FINANCE CORP
The country's leading charge card specialists

PRESS RELEASE
(for immediate publication)
Credi-Card Working Around The Clock This Christmas

December 7th

Credi-card's customer assistance teams will be joining the thousands of workers eating their Christmas pudding and stuffed turkey at their desks this year as the country's largest credit card company offers a 24 hour customer helpline service throughout the festive period. Some of the enquiries they expect to deal with are far from straightforward.

Examples of calls to Credi-card assistance teams range from cardholders asking: "Is Tesco's supermarket open in Tuxford on a Sunday?; what is the difference between hard and soft contact lenses?; what are the winning lottery numbers? and 'can you tell me which hotel my husband is staying at this weekend?'

Phil Jenkins, manager in charge of Credi-card's customer helpline section in Dunston says: "Some of the more unusual calls that the customer assistance teams receive from cardholders at all hours of the day include a lady calling at 3.30 am complaining that she couldn't sleep and asking if she could be sent a bundle of Credi-card leaflets to read!"

While Credi-card could not help with all these requests, the teams will be on hand to deal with more usual calls such as arranging credit limit increases, giving out account balances, changes of address, the re-issue of PIN numbers and reports of cards lost or stolen. Last year some 350 card holders made calls to Credi-card on Christmas Day and the phone teams are expecting a similar number of enquiries this year.

Credi-card customer can call the telephone number on the top of their monthly statement to contact customer assistance for general enquiries. If a cardholder needs to report their cards missing, the Credi-card lost and stolen number is 02344 4637771.

(Ends)

For further information contact: Abi Rhodes, Public Relations Dept, Credi-card Finance Corp, Tel: 02461 8374223

Press Release Example 2 : The Bad

DUNSTON COLLEGE
13 Academic Road,
Dunston New Town.

17th March

PRESS RELEASE

Dr. Jennifer Combes, the first woman President of the National College of Dieticians and currently chairperson of the Standing Conference on the Abuse of Additives, has been elected as Principal of Dunston College, Stapleford, from next autumn. She will succeed Mrs Elaine Rowntree, who is retiring.

A graduate of St. Paul's College, Sedgwick, Dr. Combes, aged 38, has been a Consultant Physician at Tuxford General Hospital since 1981, a Governmental consultant on additives since 1985 and a senior lecturer in eating disorders at Tuxford Medical College since 1990.

Her career has provided her with various managerial roles as well as membership of several influential Government dietary inquiries, including the Hutchings Report on Teenage Bulimia. Her work has been published in numerous medical and academic journals.

Dr. Combes, who is single, is a keen cello player and helps to organise the annual Tuxford Music Festival. Her other interests include wine, travel and medieval tapestries.

For further information, please contact: Jane Welford, Press Officer on 03733 2745333 ex 234.

Now, although I've labelled this as 'bad' this press release is well constructed and holds most of the necessary information for a reporter to be able to knock out a few paragraphs. The question is: *would a news-editor see past the dullness of it*? There is a guaranteed yawn in every sentence.

It might well be that Dr. Combes, contrary to the impression given here, is actually a lively character with a ready wit. The chances are that we'll never find out. A news-editor will see this as a three-paragraph filler rather than a tip-off for a potential personality piece.

Press Release Example 3 : The Ugly

URGENT ANNOUNCEMENT

Multi-tron Industries Ltd. are rightfully proud that the Multi-trex 2,000 is entering the second initiative phase of its development schedule - a full quarter ahead of predictions.

Company executive Mr Hedges said: "We are all proud that the Mutli-trex 2,000 is going into its second initiative phase ahead of predictions. This goes to prove that the on-going development review outlined in our January objective statement was correct and our critics were wrong and had nothing to fear."

The 2,000, an upgrade on the 1500, is hoped to sell to an expanding and appreciative audience. Mr Hedges added: "We will be a world beater. There is no doubt about that. The 2,000 has every feature that our customers have asked for - it is state of the art, using the latest technology and information delivery systems." It is hoped that the 2,000 will be on sale in selected outlets sometimes in the next two-year promotional cycle.

Well, where do you begin to unravel an awful press release like this? You may think this is an extreme example, but handouts like this land on news-editors' desks everyday. Vague, devoid of information and packed with jargon, such press releases are worse than useless. Not surprisingly they *always* end up in the bin.

The list of unanswered questions is endless. Who are Multi-tron Industries? Are they local? What do they produce? Where is their factory? What is the Multi-trex 2,000? What does second initiation phase of its development programme mean? A quarter of what ahead of predictions? Whose predictions? What critics? And so on. The press release is almost incomprehensible but the crime is compounded by the fact that we aren't told what title the mysterious Mr Hedges holds or whether he even has a Christian name. The reporter can't even ring up and ask because there is no phone number or contact name given.

The news-editor who received this gibberish wouldn't bother reading past the first paragraph. And I don't blame him. Do you?

CHAPTER SEVEN

BEST TIME TO CONTACT
A NEWSDESK

Even having the right contacts and making a good impression aren't necessarily enough to guarantee you'll get your story into the newspapers or broadcast over the airwaves.

The timing of your approach is crucial. Success depends not only on the time of year you send in your story, but even hinges on the day of the week or the hour of the day you ring up! All news outfits have quiet spells and chaotic times. It's up to you to discover what times should be avoided and learn when there is likely to be a news drought - when scarcities of stories gives you an opening to gain extra publicity.

7.1 DO YOUR RESEARCH
Busy times vary from newspaper to newspaper, from radio station to TV studio. To ensure you know the best time to talk to a news-editor, ring up the switchboard and ask. The operator

puts through all the calls and will know when the newsdesk has quieter moments.

Ask the newsdesk when they like to be contacted, and when to avoid. Make a note of it. If you already have good links with reporters, you may find that they have their own quiet time when they make a point of escaping the turmoil for a relaxing coffee at the cafe across the road. See if they'll let you join them for a chat. You'll find them more open and responsive to ideas if they don't have phones ringing in their ears and a news-editor yelling at them!

7.2 AVOID CHAOTIC TIMES

The nearer you get to a newspaper's edition being printed or a radio or TV news bulletin being broadcast, the more frantic and rushed things become in the newsroom. Urgent last minute phone calls are made by reporters, keyboards clatter, facts are checked and double checked, news-editors hurriedly scan stories for mistakes and missed angles, and everyone stares at the clock as the minutes whisk by.

It's a foolhardy person who rings up at this point expecting a newsdesk to pay him more than scant attention. This is the worst of all possible times to ring or turn up with a story idea. You may even find yourself being turned away with the promise that: *"We'll get back to you when things get quieter"*.

Don't let it happen to you. Find out what times your local paper prints its editions and make note of TV and radio bulletin times.

Don't ring up during a TV bulletin or main programme - it's likely that the whole newsroom will stop working to watch the broadcast. Some switchboards won't put through your calls while a news programme is being broadcast.

7.3 GUARANTEED 'BAD' TIMES
Evening Newspapers
As a rule, it's not a good idea to contact an evening newspaper in the mornings unless you have an urgent breaking story.

Reporters will be busy writing stories for that day's paper and won't be free to deal with less urgent items until the afternoon.

Don't ring up in the evening. Most newsdesks aren't manned after 6 pm and you'll be asked to call back the next day. It's possible that the office will be completely empty and the phone won't be answered. Those reporters who are working, will be out on interviews or away covering such things as evening council meetings. Many evening papers are unmanned on Sundays.

Nationals and regional morning papers

Afternoons are also the best time to contact national newspapers and regional morning newspapers. As journalists work through the evening and into the night to produce these papers, you may find that the specialist writer you need doesn't turn up until lunch time the next day.

Even if the newsdesk is manned from early on, it's possible that there will only be sufficient reporters in the morning to cover urgent breaking stories.

Staff will be there in the evenings, but will be extremely busy and may be reluctant to talk to you. On regional morning papers, the newsdesk may close down after 8 pm. After that, all calls will be fielded by a 'duty' reporter. The chances are he'll ask you to call back the next day.

Weeklies and Sunday papers

As they only publish once a week, national Sunday papers and local weekly papers have their own work 'cycle'. With Sunday papers, work doesn't begin until half way through the week, culminating in a flurry of activity on a Saturday evening.

It's unlikely that you will find anyone in the office on a Monday. It's also unlikely that you will find many staff working outside office hours until the latter part of the week. Saturday is a bad time to ring with any story that isn't urgent.

Weekly papers have a similar cycle but they tend to run from Wednesday to Wednesday. Many local weeklies are delivered to the newsagents on a Thursday morning, after being printed on Wednesday night.

This means that staff will have worked late on the Wednesday and will probably not turn up until lunch time on the Thursday. If you have a story idea, Thursday afternoon is the best time to make an approach and Wednesday afternoon is the worst possible.

Because local papers have smaller staffs, it can be that a reporter who had to work late one night is allowed to have a lie in and come in later the next morning. So phoning after 10 am can be a good idea.

TV and radio

Regional TV and radio stations newsdesks tend to operate to normal office hours. After 6 pm, and at weekends, you're liable to find yourself talking to a duty reporter rather than the news-editor.

One important point to remember is that regional TV stations broadcast their main news programme between 6 pm and 7 pm. The latter half of the afternoon will be geared to making sure all the late breaking stories are ready to broadcast so it's a bad time to try to contact specific reporters - they may be tied up doing last-minute editing.

If it's the news-editor you want, it's worth trying after 4 pm. By then his 'same-day' work will be over and he'll be looking at the next day's story list, deciding where to send next morning's camera crews.

If he's not available, and your story isn't urgent, ask to be put through to the 'forward planner'. This is a journalist who compiles a long-term diary of future events worth the news-editor's attention.

7.4 DEADLINES

Every page, every edition, every programme and every bulletin will have its own deadlines - cut-off points when the news stories must be finished and ready for sub-editors to process.

Even though an evening paper's first edition might not print until 1 pm, the deadlines for the inside pages might be several hours earlier. Miss those and your story - unless urgent enough to warrant going on the front page - will have to wait until the next day.

Find out the deadlines (last copy times) for all editions and bulletins. Don't make the mistake of contacting a news organisation too late for it to be able to print the story!

For example, there's no point ringing up the environment reporter on a Wednesday if that's the day the column appears. It was probably sub-edited and laid-out the day before. Your item will have to be held over until the next week.

7.5 PLAN PUBLICITY IN ADVANCE

Many people miss out on coverage because they simply contact a newspaper too late. They don't give the news-editor adequate notice. Publicity is the last item on their list of priorities and is often tackled as an after-thought.

If you've been planning a carnival for three months, it's silly to leave it until an hour before the grand opening to ring up your local paper to tell them. You've had more than 90 days in which to make contact - why leave it until the last moment?

It's crazy but people do this - in their thousands. News-editors and chief photographers lose count of the number of times they have a phone call from club organisers saying: *"We're having a pensioners' party this afternoon and we thought it would nice if you could send a reporter and photographer to cover it."*

The answer is usually no - because there's no one available. It's sad, but all too often people who've rung up too late feel slighted - as though the newspaper isn't interested in them. They can feel that a rival organisation is getting preferential treatment. The reality is, the rival club probably alerted the newsdesk a month before the event they wanted covered.

7.6 GET INTO THE DIARY

To appreciate why there are no staff available to cover events at the last minute, you have to understand the mechanics of news-gathering.

Although spectacular unexpected events like fires, car crashes and disasters get the biggest headlines, they make up a very small percentage of the news that is printed or broadcast. Most news will be coverage of routine, planned, events - council meetings, weddings, prize givings, open days, product launches, trials, celebrity visits, supermarket openings and the like.

The newsdesk will have been informed of these events - maybe weeks in advance. Based on this information, the news-editor will have made a judgment about which story will be worth a reporter's time.

When these events are chosen, details are entered into the relevant day's page of a large desk diary. One of the news-editor's last tasks of the afternoon is to look at the next day's diary entries and decide which reporter will be sent out to cover which event.

Apart from one or two reporters who will be 'off diary' - kept in reserve to work on particular news stories or to be available to rush out to fires and car crashes - most staff will have a full day's work allocated to them.

The news-editor won't have any staff free to cover a routine event where the organisers didn't give him any advance notice. He certainly won't take a reporter off a major news story to go to a carnival or an open day.

One harsh fact of life is that there are more events happening in a town than can ever be covered in person by reporters or photographers. Publicity can be a matter of who gives the paper the most notice.

7.7 CRASHES TAKE PRIORITY

All news outfits have limited reporting resources. If a major car crash or fire occurs, a reporter or photographer may be pulled off a routine 'diary' job to cover the accident.

Even though you were expecting a journalist to attend your event he may be diverted to a serious breaking story. It may be disappointing, but it is unavoidable.

To help minimise the risk of letting you down, a news-editor will always point out that a reporter will try his best to attend your event - *but he can't promise*.

7.8 EXPLOIT OPPORTUNITIES

Be smart - give yourself an edge. Find out when news outfits are likely to be short of stories and approach them when they are frantically searching for material. Your phone call may come as an answer to a prayer for a news-editor urgently trying to fill a huge paper during a slack news day.

Not only will you be guaranteed more column inches than usual, but you may find that the news-editor's news judgment or quality criteria goes out the window. An item that wouldn't thrill a news-editor on Monday may be viewed by him as a nugget of gold several days later when his in-tray is empty and he has only two reporters on duty.

Even if there are no good news stories around, he still has to find a front page lead and main stories for all the inside pages. In those circumstances, virtually any story becomes a good story.

7.9 BE A LIFE-SAVER!

Now, unless you work in the building you won't know when illness or holidays reduce the size of a paper's reporting staff. Neither will you know when the level of advertising rises so high that an editor suddenly has to increase the number of pages in his paper to maintain the 50/50 or 60/40 ratio between advertisements and editorial content. The chances are the editorial department won't know until just the afternoon before, so no-one outside will have a clue that there is more news space to fill.

But, although you aren't there to take advantage of these sudden news-flow hiccups, you can do the next best thing and let journalist contacts know that they can always ring for a story - and you'll always oblige.

A 'contact' who can manufacture a story out of thin air is a reporter's dream. A press officer who can get a reporter out of a bind while winning extra publicity for his organisation, is guaranteed a lorry-load of friends.

7.10 HOW DO YOU SPOT OPPORTUNITIES?

Even if you don't have a direct link to your local newsdesk, there are certain signs you can look for that show a paper is short of stories and would welcome your news.

- Is your local paper suddenly carrying a lot more national news than usual? If this happens over several consecutive days, this could mean that there aren't enough local stories or that the paper is short-staffed. In those circumstances an editor will fall back on the services of a national news agency such as The Press Association to provide him with copy.
- Is the paper suddenly printing more feature material - articles, showbiz news, cookery, write-ups on holidays, films, cars, fashion etc. - and cutting back on the number of column inches given over to hard news?
- Is it suddenly printing pages of photographs where normally it would print several news stories?
- Are the stories being given over-elaborate lay-out with maps, graphics, extra pictures, larger headlines etc. - all designed to eat up editorial space?
- Is the paper suddenly giving over space to nostalgia pictures - old scenes of the town, extracts from the archives? Has it started devoting more space to competitions or for 'in-house' advertisements for its own promotional products such as key-rings, special souvenir editions, tee-shirts, posters, or pens?
- Are there large *'Coming Next Week'* blurbs giving details of supplements and features in future editions? A few such blurbs may not signify anything, but if more than one is used in an edition - eating up lots of space - it may be a clue.
- Are stories starting to carry a sentence on the end saying: *'What Do You Think About This Issue? Drop Us A Line And We'll Print Your Comments'*. The chances are this device to encourage reader feedback is being used to generate editorial 'copy'.
- Has the paper actually made an appeal for stories? It does happen. Few editors will admit they are short of news to print, but they may disguise this by asking the public for more news

from a certain part of the 'patch', more news from certain age groups or more news on specific topics such as the environment, health or good citizenship. *'Have You Got A Super Neighbour? Write In And Let Us Know'.*

- If the paper is covering a big, long-running story such as a murder trial or a planning inquiry, it may be that the news-editor will be desperate to find other lighter, more cheery, news to print to even the balance. This may be your chance for coverage.

He may have to keep several reporters tied up for months covering the major story and the other journalists may be hard-pushed to fill the remaining news pages. You may actually be doing them a favour to suggest a story that can be easily researched with just one short interview.

7.11 REGULAR 'HEADACHE' TIMES
Although short-term news flow problems may hit one particular paper at one specific time, there are times of the year when *all* news outfits struggle to fill their pages and bulletins.

Bank Holidays
These are a particularly awkward time for news-editors. It's likely that in the days leading up to a Bank Holiday Weekend papers will be thick - the pagination pushed up by the large number of leisure adverts for theme parks, stately homes, museums, bowling alleys, ice rinks, cinemas, restaurants and pubs, coach tours, boat trips and countless craft fairs, car boot sales and fetes.

These thick papers will eat up any stockpile of stories and pictures, leaving the news-editor's cupboard almost bare. As journalists, like everyone else, want to be out enjoying themselves in the sun, the paper will probably run over the holiday weekend on a skeleton staff.

Reporters will be able to generate enough editorial copy by covering the carnivals, shows and motor rallies to fill the papers printed over the holiday weekend (including the Monday). But this material won't replenish the stockpile or go any serious way towards filling the papers for the next few days. It can be the following weekend before the supply of stories is back to normal.

So for the period from immediately before a Bank Holiday to several days after, a newsdesk is likely to welcome your story.

Papers aren't the only news medium affected. Although radio and TV stations don't have to cope with this huge increase in demand for material, they do try to run skeleton news staffs over the Bank Holiday. Their reporters also have to put up with the massive inconvenience of being unable to get in touch with MP's, councillors, senior police, fire and ambulance officers and many other potential interviewees because contacts are away enjoying the break.

Even if a newsdesk has an emergency contact number for the press departments of large companies, public bodies or the emergency services, a reporter is likely to be put through to a 'duty' press officer who will field the enquiry as best he can - but may not be able to do more than issue a bland: *"We're looking into it"* statement.

This difficulty in getting hold of people can reduce the number and type of stories radio and TV stations run over a Bank Holiday. If you ring up with a sensible story idea - that is easy to cover, lending itself to good TV pictures - you may strike lucky and find a camera crew winging its way to you.

The silly season
News-editors dread the summer months. It can seem as if the whole country has gone away on holiday. Schools and colleges close, the football season ends, factories stop production, council and other statutory bodies don't hold meetings and even the most publicity hungry politician is lazing on a Mediterranean beach.

It's no surprise that this period is known as the silly season, because in the desperate rush to fill empty pages any story that can be printed, will be printed - no matter how silly or ridiculous it appears. It's as if news-editors lose all sense of reason.

Talking dogs, UFO sightings, crop circles, the annual reappearance of the Loch Ness Monster, exclusive interviews with Lord Lucan - all these and more fill the front pages of our daily newspapers. Even national TV and radio go for quirky, off-the-wall, news items in a bid to fill bulletins. After all, with parliament in recess, they've lost their main source of scandal, intrigue, rows and blazing arguments.

Astute PR people know that this is the ideal time to launch a new product or get their celebrity clients into the headlines. Coverage is guaranteed.

If it works for the rich and famous, why shouldn't it work for you? Even if the news-editor of your local radio station hasn't yet been reduced to stories on mysterious giant cats stalking sheep in the neighbourhood, he'll probably be delighted to give you plenty of air time.

The Yuletide 'dead' zone

Bank Holidays are a headache for newsdesks, but these problems are enormously magnified when applied to the increasing long holidays taken over Christmas and New Year.

Many people take two full weeks holiday and some businesses close up on Christmas Eve and don't re-open until the second or third of January.

This period is a dead zone for news gathering, and skeleton editorial staffs will have to dig hard to find any story worth putting out. As well as being hard to contact, most people aren't doing anything news-worthy. They're busy having a wild time at parties, visiting relatives or relaxing with their feet up in front of an old movie on the television.

Even professional public relations firms are closed over the Yuletide break so that the flow of potential stories all but dries up. TV and radio stations reduce the number of bulletins and shorten their duration. Newspapers are thin and full of 'features'. What news there is will probably come from phone calls to the control rooms of the fire, ambulance and police and will heavily feature road smashes, minor crime and fires.

All rely strongly on round-ups of the year - looking back at the highlights of the last twelve months or use 'light-weight' pieces such as asking local celebrities what their New Year's resolutions are.

During this dearth of stories, you'll find little difficulty in getting coverage. If you have a good gritty story that can make a front-page lead, you will be welcomed by a news-editor like a long-lost friend.

The only day to avoid in the dead zone is New Year's Day. As well as having photographs of babies born in the first minutes of January 1st, the paper will be able to fill most of its space requirements with news of local people who have received titles and awards in the New Year's Honours List.

CHAPTER EIGHT

HANDLING PRESS ENQUIRIES

RULE Nº 1 :

" DON'T PANIC "

HELLO! MR WILLIAMS,
IT'S 'THE TIMES' HERE....
· · · ° · · · · · MR WILLIAMS?
HELLO ?...HELLO? · · · · ·
· · · · · · · · HELLO ?· · · · ·

Simon '96

Although it is comparatively easy to be in control of the news you put out - choosing where, when and how you contact a newsdesk, it's not so easy to cope when a news organisation contacts you for a quote or an interview.

Would you know what to do if a reporter rang you up out of the blue, concerning a story you knew nothing about? Could you react quickly to get what information was needed? Would you go to pieces and miss the opportunity for free publicity?

All too often clubs, businesses and charities are caught on the hop because a reporter needs to know a simple fact and they can't provide it. Don't let it happen to you!

8.1 CALL BACKS

If a newsdesk gets in touch as a result of a handout you've submitted or a phone call you've made, they'll expect you to be able to react immediately. You should be ready, well briefed and alert to handle any and all queries and know exactly where you can find the necessary information. You should also have people available to supply quotes and help explain any technical or scientific concepts.

8.2 PRESS OFFICERS

Appoint one person as a press officer and supply that individual's name, address, and day/ night-time phone numbers to all news organisations in your area. Make sure that the person you select is easily contactable - there's no point in picking a press officer who isn't on the phone. Likewise, don't pick someone who is frequently out of town on business. Ensure that the press officer is never far from a phone - buy them a mobile if necessary. And don't select someone whose phone is going to be constantly engaged.

8.3 CHANNELLING ENQUIRIES

It is important that you channel all information through your press officer so that newspapers know who to ring, confident that all their enquiries will be dealt with quickly and comprehensively. Reporters often ring up on a breaking story with only an hour to gather information. Delays are a major headache - especially when the information sought should be easily and readily available.

8.4 ADVANTAGES TO JOURNALISTS

Having one person - and one person only - to contact per organisation is an enormous help for journalists. All such names go into the office 'contacts' books - one of the most useful reference books a reporter can use. Its entries eliminate much wasted time in ringing round trying to track down 'spokesmen' and allows reporters more time to ensure they get the story right.

8.5 ADVANTAGES TO YOU

The benefits to you are just as great. Having a recognised press liaison officer means that you can restrict what information is given out. If every member of your organisation knows that John Smith is the only one authorised to handle media enquiries, then there is a greatly reduced risk of someone saying the wrong thing to the wrong person at the wrong time.

Staff will sometimes give out wrong information in a genuine attempt to be helpful. Others, flustered by the urgency and insistence of a reporter can be pushed into making 'unfortunate' statements - often unaware of the impact of what they're saying.

For example, on one occasion a reporter rang a council official to gather information for an 'inoffensive' feature article he was doing on the parks department. The moment he mentioned the word parks to him, the official started to mumble that it wasn't his fault that various lawns hadn't been mowed for weeks. The firm sub-contracted to do the work had let him down.

Now, that official - unused to dealing with reporters - had made the assumption that the journalist knew all about his lawn problems and was putting together a story on it. Of course, the reporter didn't know anything about it until the council man opened his mouth. His desire to put over fulsome excuses - including various facts and figures which helped his own personal case - gave the journalist a story!

8.6 AVOIDING LEAKS

Having one authorised spokesman ensures there are no accidental 'leaks', and guarantees that only one message is given out. It can be damaging for different people in the same small firm to make contradictory statements - even if the topic being discussed seems outwardly innocent.

Imagine the dismay of having reporters ringing up your firm to ask about the new £1m international order you've landed for machine parts and being told by your sales manager that he is delighted at the success, but your production manager tells them he is upset because he thought the order was going to be larger.

As the disappointment angle is stronger, that's the one most likely to appear in print. Inevitably, the firm that has placed this lucrative work with you is none too pleased to hear that their patronage is 'upsetting and disappointing' to you!

8.7 WHO TO CHOOSE?

It's vital that you don't allow sentimentality or club politics to influence your choice. It's no good picking the club chairman just because he thinks it is a glamorous role and should rightly be his. If he isn't the best possible person to field press enquiries then don't pick him. It's better to have a chairman whose ego gets a little bruised than have your club look foolish by giving out wrong information or creating a bad impression.

Take a tip from large firms. If their managing director comes across badly on screen or has a habit of putting his foot in his mouth, they make sure their public relations team handle the press.

There's nothing more infuriating for a hard-pressed reporter than to ring up a club president and have him dither about because he doesn't know exactly what to say but is too embarrassed to admit it.

8.8 CONSOLATION PRIZE

Also, don't look upon the press officer's job as a 'consolation prize' to be given to a committee stalwart who fails to be elected as treasurer or secretary. It is a vital role and a great deal of thought should go into selecting the right man for the job. It is more than just an impressive title on a club letterhead. Unfortunately, some clubs appoint press officers who've never spoken to a reporter in their lives and wouldn't even begin to know how to handle a media enquiry.

8.9 WHAT MAKES A GOOD PRESS OFFICER?

Your media spokesperson doesn't need to be a power-suited, fax-hungry spin doctor with an eye on every angle - just someone with a level head, a good phone manner and a pleasant personality.

Dealing with enquiries can be daunting for the inexperienced, so it's not a good idea to pick someone lacking in confidence or easily flustered. Make sure that the individual is a volunteer because having an unhelpful, frightened or resentful person forced to deal with the media is worse than having no press officer at all.

Your press officer is your ambassador, projecting the image of your company or club which the public will see and judge you by, so make sure he is bright, articulate and fully conversant with the role he's being asked to take on. Common-sense, a positive attitude and good organisational skills are vital.

8.10 ON THE LOOK-OUT

A 'switched-on' press officer is more than just someone who fields enquiries and puts out handouts when asked. He should think like a reporter and always be on the look-out for a good story that can be pitched to a paper or TV station.

He should see the publicity potential in company or club activities - finding stories that ordinary employees or club members wouldn't necessarily spot - and be able to lure the media with a carefully chosen 'hook'.

A press officer should be hungry for coverage, constantly thinking up new ways to get his group into the headlines. To do this he has to be at the centre of things - he must know what everyone is doing if you expect him to spot publicity opportunities.

Because news goes stale so rapidly, he must be free to act quickly. There's no point having a press officer if he has to wait until the next company board meeting or club committee get-together before he can get permission to ring news-editors.

If you do allow your press officer the freedom to act on his own initiative, you have to be confident of his judgment - another good reason for ensuring you select the right person for the role. It's a job with enormous responsibilities.

8.11 GOOD NEWS-SENSE

Your press officer must have good news sense. This isn't a skill that can be developed overnight, but a good press officer will study newspapers and broadcasts to get a feel for what interests news-editors.

He'll closely study how stories he's given the local media have been used and see what rival groups have done to get maximum news coverage. He'll know that news stories don't have to have earth-shattering significance to be printed, but must have a quirky or attention-grabbing quality. He'll fully understand 'angles' and the best way to slant material to make it intriguing.

8.12 GET TO KNOW HOW THE MEDIA WORKS

Your press officer can't hope to be effective if he doesn't understand how different news media are organised, their different news values and how they gather stories. He must know the type of information and co-operation they'll expect when they ring up. So anyone taking on the role for the first time should do his homework and read up on the subject.

Many newspapers and TV stations run organised tours and these are an invaluable way of peeking behind the scenes. Most of the background information needed is given in the guide's commentary and it helps if your press officer has a 'taste' of what it's like in a busy newsroom.

Even if your local paper, radio or TV station doesn't run a tour, it's worth ringing up to ask if someone from the editorial department can spare half-an-hour to take your press officer round and explain how news-gathering works. Most media organisations are only too pleased to oblige, and will give useful advice on the best way to deal with their own individual requirements.

8.13 MAKE CONTACTS

To be effective, a good press officer will have built up solid links with local journalists. They should be happy to contact him, knowing he can deliver the facts and quotes they need for their stories.

When appointed, the first thing your press officer should do is write to all the local news organisations to introduce himself.

Even if this fails to stir much of a reaction, his name, phone number and address will go on file in the contacts book.

He should ring and make an appointment to meet various news-editors and reporters. He should suggest having a brief chat over a drink or a cup of coffee. He should expect to be the one who pays for the drinks - remembering that news-editors don't need him, but he needs them!

Get him to explain what your group does, have him say he'll always be happy to help out with any reporter's queries and have him find out how best to submit your stories.

He should aim to make friends with journalists. By taking an interest, he'll show he's serious about the job he's been given and is keen to be as professional as possible. An efficient press officer won't pester, but will stay in touch on a regular basis.

8.14 USE A PROFESSIONAL

If you are lucky enough to have a club or charity member who is also a journalist, then press him into action. Ask if he will act as your press officer. Most journalists are only too willing to help out any group they know well.

As a member of the media, he'll know exactly when newspapers, TV and radio stations are short on 'copy' and looking for stories that can be covered easily. He'll be able to tailor your story to fit these gaps, and will be able to write a handout in a fraction of the time it would take anyone else.

He'll instinctively know what angle will most interest editors and will ensure that all the necessary facts are available. This may mean him interviewing other club members to gather information and quotes before making any approach to a news outlet. He'll also be able to judge if the story you're trying to place is worth a newspaper's valuable column inches.

8.15 PULLING STRINGS

It is unlikely that a journalist will deliberately pull strings for you - no matter how involved he is in your club. But, he *will* have natural advantages over his 'amateur' press officer counterparts, which will pay dividends.

The chances are that he'll probably already know all the news-editors in the area and be on first-name terms with many of them. Being used to discussing stories on the phone, he'll sound confident and well briefed. He'll be viewed as a friend worth speaking to - not as a stranger and potential time waster.

Armed with intimate knowledge of each news chief's likes and dislikes, pet hates and idiosyncrasies, your press officer will know what type of sales pitch to use. Ask any angler and he'll tell you - half the secret is knowing what bait to use to hook your fish.

8.16 SPEAKING THE LINGO

As well as having inside knowledge, your professional press officer will have the advantage of speaking the same language as the people he's trying to interest. There will be a natural rapport between people with shared values and outlook, and a news-editor will look more favourably on a story brought to him by another newsman. He knows a journalist won't bother him with trivia or ideas that are unsuitable or wrongly targeted.

It goes beyond merely seeing things the same way. News-editor and press officer literally speak the same lingo. Like the legal profession, journalism has its own language - a mixture of slang, technical jargon and barrack room camaraderie - and it's difficult for someone outside the business to learn to speak like a native.

As well as being able to convince a news-editor that a story is worth covering, a journalist press officer will be able to discuss whether a story is a potential splash (front page lead), page lead (main story on an inside page), a nib (a news in brief filler) or a hamper or anchor (the horizontal stories that run across the top and bottom of the page). He'll be aware of any photographic opportunities and will be able to discuss potential pictures with the newsdesk or chief photographer.

8.17 CONTACT CALL-UP

You don't have to be in the news for a newspaper to get in touch with you. When news is thin on the ground, a paper still has pages to fill and reporters will be instructed to ring round their contacts to see if they can dig up any stories.

Your press officer may be contacted to see if your club or business is planning any special events which you haven't yet got round to publicising. He may be asked to give updated details on a long-term project you're running.

When papers are actively seeking news, you are guaranteed good coverage - so always be on the alert to make full use of the opportunity.

Don't say: *"Sorry, we haven't got anything happening at the moment"*, think what you might want to publicise in the near future. Maybe, it's worth discussing a project that's only in the initial planning phase - as long as you don't give away any commercially sensitive information or upset partners who haven't yet been fully consulted.

8.18 LOCAL ANGLE

Provincial newspapers are always seeking to find local angles on national stories, and that often means ringing up regional representatives of national organisations to get the local story.

For example, if there is a drought and river levels drop dramatically risking fish stocks, your evening paper will ring up the angling clubs in its circulation area to find out if they've been affected. If you're the press officer of such a club, you'd be expected to provide a few paragraphs of quotes saying whether fish stocks were, in your opinion, low.

Similarly, if a national report showed that small firms were suffering most under a tax change, the paper might well ring half a dozen local firms to find out what they thought. These are Heaven-sent opportunities to gain free publicity. Don't allow them to go to someone else because you weren't able to reply in time.

8.19 UNUSUAL REQUESTS

Reporters often ring up to ask for the most bizarre sounding things. They may want to do a feature article on potholing and need your caving club to take them underground. They might ask your class of cookery students to take part in a spoof Masterchef competition.

If the unusual request is feasible, why not go along with it? Don't be scared off just because the idea is a little different from the norm. Not only will you get great coverage, but you might even enjoy it!

It doesn't have to be hard to organise. One firm of steeplejacks working on a church tower landed themselves a full page of free publicity by allowing a reporter to climb up their ladders to the top of the spire. The article, which took only half-an-hour to arrange, gave the firm nearly £1,000 of free advertising!

Press photographers are always on the lookout for quirky, eye-catching picture opportunities. The more outrageous the better. If your hotel is starting a series of murder mystery weekends, you may be asked to dress up the staff in Agatha Christie-style costumes and be snapped in 'Cluedo' poses. Join in the fun. Be a good sport. Publicity can be priceless. Don't turn it down when it's offered!

CHAPTER NINE

THE PROFESSIONAL TOUCH

You don't have to be a 'pro' or a publicity whizz-kid to get the occasional bit of media coverage.

But what if you want more than just a few lines in your local paper? What if you need to have a carefully planned publicity campaign that can't rely on a few hit-and-miss mentions and the occasional headline?

Regular, sustained publicity, is more tricky to get - but it is possible if you make media relations and news management a central strand of your activities.

This chapter looks at ways of being more professional about seeking coverage - making publicity a certainty.

9.1 PRESS CONFERENCE

If you have a story which will interest many different news outfits, you may find yourself spending literally days being interviewed. You'll be unable to get on with your work and you'll get to the point where you cringe at being asked the same questions over and over.

It's far easier to "get it all over with" in one morning by inviting all the interested journalists to a press conference or media briefing. You can then read out your information, show off any new product and answer questions in front of an audience - instead of giving a series of one-on-one interviews.

Although facing several rows of faces might, at first, seem intimidating, it is far easier than trying to keep your replies fresh and lively when you're on the twentieth individual interview!

9.2 STAY RELAXED

Don't be scared at the thought of organising a press conference. It doesn't have to be a high-profile media event with banks of microphones and snazzy designer backdrops. The boardroom or canteen of most companies will double up as a press briefing room. If you don't have a room that's suitable, most hotels have conference rooms for hire.

Look upon the briefing as just another business meeting. Keep it informal and light-hearted. Chat to the reporters and camera crews beforehand to see what they need from you.

9.3 CONFERENCE CHECKLIST

Give some advance thought to the press conference venue, timing and details. It's often difficult to change the arrangements on the day. Go through the following checklist to ensure that you've covered everything.

- Make sure you've invited everyone you think will be interested. Send a written invitation to the briefing and follow this up with a phone call to the newsdesk to check that their reporter will be coming.
- Check that the conference is being held at a convenient time for TV coverage. Don't hold a conference late in the morning when it will miss the lunch time bulletins or too late in the afternoon when it will miss the main tea-time programme.

- Make sure the room you intend to use is big enough to accommodate everyone comfortably. Remember that TV cameras need an unobstructed view of the speaker's podium or desk.
- Check that the venue is suitable - that it is easy to find, has adequate parking, seating, toilets, telephones and plenty of power points!
- Make sure the room you've picked is near to the parking zone. Camera crews won't be happy if they have to carry heavy equipment all the way through a factory.
- Check that the room is in a quiet part of the building, has good acoustics and is well away from main roads, airports or noisy factories. Traffic rumble carries for some distance.
- Make sure the room has good natural light, and that there is adequate artificial lighting.
- Check that all the main speakers have a microphone. A press conference can be noisy and it is important that every word you say is heard clearly.
- Have tea and coffee ready for journalists as they arrive. This is more than just politeness. While reporters have coffee, camera crews have the time to set up and it gives you a chance to iron out any last-minute snags before the conference begins.
- Always have prepared handouts and press packs of pictures and other relevant material. If the conference is going to be long or involve detailed technical explanations, it saves the reporter taking down screeds of copious notes. He can concentrate on noting the answers you give to questions.
- Have extra copies of the press packs lying on a table near the exit. It is likely that by the end of the briefing someone will have lost his pack and need a replacement.
- Be prepared for radio and TV journalists to ask you for short supplementary interviews after the main conference is over. These will usually only last a few minutes. TV journalists may want to 'shoot' you against a particular background and radio reporters may want to interview you where the sound quality is better. Try to make sure you have a quiet ante-room where

you can be interviewed away from the noise of the main conference hall.

9.4 AWARENESS WEEKS

Special theme awareness weeks are becoming increasingly popular - especially with charities and pressure groups. By designating a particular week in the year as Healthy Eating Week or Cancer Awareness Week, it is easier to gain media coverage for these causes.

Such publicity is highly effective. Instead of having a piecemeal approach - with various assorted stories and feature articles appearing haphazardly throughout the year, dotted around the different news media - publicity is channelled and tightly targeted. Not only are numerous stories printed in a short space of time, but they appear simultaneously across the whole spectrum of news outlets.

The effect is the same as an advertising campaign costing hundreds of thousands of pounds. Newsdesks like awareness weeks because they provide a 'peg' to hang stories on. Reporters like the weeks because covering stories is easy - charities put on special events, make people available for interview and produce detailed press packs and handouts.

9.5 SPIN-OFFS

Groups who organise awareness weeks benefit from spin-offs. Usually there isn't the room in a news story to explain the background to major social issues or look at the causes and impact of diseases on sufferers. But an awareness week gives newspaper feature departments the chance to run analytical 'backgrounder' articles and encourages radio and TV stations to broadcast short mini-documentaries.

Newspapers and television companies will sometimes work with local charities to produce awareness week information packs which are offered to readers/viewers. Radio stations will often run phone-ins and invite those running the awareness week to have a special slot to talk about the aims of their charity or campaign and the need to increase public awareness of the work they do.

9.6 RUNNING AN AWARENESS WEEK

It's vital that you are well prepared. Make sure you have produced detailed press material and have experts on hand to be interviewed. The week can be hectic, with numerous reporters ringing up for stories, radio producers asking you to supply panel members for discussion shows and TV news-editors wanting you to stunt up events for filming - so make sure you are free. Take time off work if necessary.

Start the week with a high profile event - stage a photo opportunity, a celebrity appearance or a press conference. Don't turn down any media requests - no matter how awkward or time-consuming.

Remember: check to make sure that your awareness week doesn't clash with any other awareness weeks - especially those run by rival groups.

9.7 CHASE EVERY OPPORTUNITY

Newsdesks look for local slants on national stories, but even they can't spot every story opportunity. If you think you can offer a local angle on a national story, ring up.

A national survey may show that people are suffering from 'care fatigue' - being bombarded with so many charity appeals that even concerned people become immune to pleas for help. If your local charity branch has suffered badly because of this - or if you've been lucky and have bucked the trend - call and suggest a story.

Educationalists may claim that today's children are only interested in computers and high-tech toys, but if your toy shop does a roaring trade in traditional playthings like footballs, dolls and train sets, contact the newsdesk and suggest a story.

You might even be able to interest your regional TV station - suggest that a reporter might like to do a piece to camera kicking a football or using a hula hoop. An off-beat item like this might be a winner!

Scan the columns of national papers for stories that give your organisation an opening for 'local angle' coverage. You never know, a news-editor may have been frantically searching for someone like you to help him illustrate the story!

9.8 SUGGEST PHOTOGRAPHS

Newspapers are always on the look-out for good photograph ideas. Stories flood into a newsroom, but lively, eye-catching pictures are considerably more difficult to find. Many news-editors despair when all they are offered are static cheque-presentation pictures or line-ups of men in dinner jackets at company dinner-dances.

If you can offer the chance of a bright, interesting photograph, you will get a news-editor's attention. The picture might even convince him to give you coverage when the actual story isn't that exciting. Stress the picture side of your sales pitch. It might just click!

9.9 PHOTO OPPORTUNITIES

For television, magazines and national newspapers, often the picture *is* the story. A startling visual image is what they need to interest their audience.

Not surprisingly, many groups seeking publicity play up to this by staging photo opportunities - quirky events designed to look good in photographs or on 30 second news broadcasts.

Theatres, zoos, political parties and Royalty all know the value of the photo opportunity. Press and TV cameras will turn up for sure if an actor is frolicking about to promote a show, a zoo is showing off new-born lion cubs, a politician is wearing a silly hat to visit a biscuit factory or a Prince is posing on a snow-covered mountain.

Sometimes it seems as though an entire election campaign is nothing more than wall-to-wall photo opportunities. They are, in some ways, a cynical technique for gaining publicity. Events are stunted up - purely to lure in the lenses.

However, they *are* highly effective and shouldn't be ruled out on grounds of bad taste or frivolity. Anything that gains you publicity is good, and you don't have to go to ridiculous lengths. You don't need gimmicks - just a good picture idea.

9.10 FIND A PEG
Calendar dates
Can you link your story to an annual holiday or festival? If so, you'll stand more chance of coming up with a quirky idea that will interest a newsdesk.

If you own a French restaurant, why not run a series of Bastille Day events on July 14th and invite a reporter from your local paper to come along. If you've just opened a clock shop, invite a photographer to take a picture of you putting them all back an hour in the October switch to British Winter Time.

The opportunities for 'date tie-in' stories are countless. Just think how many festivals we celebrate - Christmas, Halloween, Easter, St. Valentine's Day, Bank Holiday Mondays, Guy Fawkes Night, Pancake Tuesday, New Year's Eve, Trafalgar Day, St. George's Day and even (in some counties with large American military bases) the 4th of July!

Anniversaries
Newsdesks love anniversary stories - is it 50 years since your scout troop was set up? Has your business been running 20 years and is having a celebration party for its employees? Milestone birthdays are a good selling point when it comes to getting good publicity.

9.11 CELEBRITIES
If you can find an actor, TV personality, famous sportsman or chart topping pop star to front your publicity campaign it guarantees media coverage. Readers and viewers are always interested in what the famous are doing.

Many charities already know the impact it can have when a famous 'face' acts as spokesman for an appeal. Donations flood in.

The moment a news-editor hears that you've got a 'celebrity' turning up to launch an event, he'll happily send a photographer and reporter. You may even get a feature writer turn up too - do put together a quick personality piece.

Admittedly, most of the really famous stars are bombarded with requests and will expect a hefty fee if they front your product launch. But you may feel the cost is worth it - the coverage will be worth a year's advertising!

If your charity or campaign touches directly on the interests of a star, he may agree to appear for free. Actors often lend their support to campaigns to save regional theatres and children's TV presenters will agree to open new play groups or hospital children's wards.

Celebrities like to help out when they can, so see if you have a star living in your locality that you could approach. Your celebrity doesn't have to be a soap opera hero - just someone that people will recognise. Why not try the news anchorman on your local TV station. If he's fronting your campaign, his TV company is more likely to publicise it!

9.12 WHIP UP A STORM

There's nothing news-editors love more than a controversy. Rows, feuds and angry debates are the lifeblood of the media. TV slanging matches generate soaring ratings and splutterings of condemnation make great front page headlines.

If you've got a product to publicise - and you don't mind a bit of excitement in your life - why not let your critics know exactly what you're doing? The louder they decry you and your business, the more column inches and air time you're guaranteed.

The biggest boost to sales of any product is to have a politician or celebrity to call for it to be banned - it's the most effective free publicity you can get. People who would never have bothered seeing your film, buying your book or listening to your record all want to see what the fuss is about.

The louder the calls for banning, the higher sales soar. After banning Relax by Frankie Goes to Hollywood, the single went straight to number one in the charts. Courtroom gagging attempts by the Government made Peter Wright's cloak and dagger book, Spycatcher, a bestseller. Would a moral outrage help your sales drive? It might be worth considering. You'll get all the publicity you can handle.

9.13 USE A PUBLIC RELATIONS FIRM

Many medium-sized companies find that they're of a size that they're regularly in the news but can't afford to employ a full-time press officer.

In these circumstances it may be worth thinking about using the services of a local public relations firm. Your own managers may be capable of dealing with press enquiries and be able to handle small-scale news releases - but for something larger like the launch of a major new product or the opening of a factory extension, you may feel happier tapping into the expertise of media professionals.

PR firms, not only have good contacts with all branches of the media, but can organise all aspects of publicity - from having your firm's logo printed on balloons to a full-scale media event.

CHAPTER TEN

GETTING THE MOST
FROM ADVERTISING

There's no beating a free 'plug' in the editorial pages of your local paper. But what if you can't interest a journalist in your story but urgently need to get your message across to potential clients or customers?

If you're paying to advertise with a newspaper, magazine or radio station you'll probably be expected to spend hundreds - maybe thousands of pounds. It's a big investment.

So how do you ensure that the advertising you pay for will reach the audience you intend? How do you know you'll get value for money? How to do you ensure your advert will have the impact you need? This chapter looks at targeting your message, getting advertising for the minimum cost with the maximum benefits.

PART ONE: FREE ADVERTISING

10.1 TRY EDITORIAL FIRST

Don't make the assumption that because you're promoting a product or a service that this automatically bars you from editorial coverage.

These days the dividing line between what constitutes a news story and what is an advert has been blurred until even experienced news-editors are unsure.

Is publicity for the opening of your new go-kart track an advert or a news story? Arguably, it's both. Any mention of the track will benefit you financially but the paper would be failing in its duty if it didn't tell its readers about a new local leisure activity they can try out.

In this case, if the paper's news-editor was reluctant to do a story on the track you might win him over by inviting him to send down a reporter and photographer to 'try it out.' Perhaps you could offer a day of free karting sessions for local under-privileged children and ask the paper to come down to cover that. The resulting story would boost your image in the community, and the cost of giving away a few free sessions would be considerably cheaper than paying for advertising.

10.2 THINK ABOUT FEATURES

Don't think just in terms of news stories produced by the paper's reporters and specialist correspondents. The features department - which produces articles, women's pages, entertainment guides, cookery columns, advice lines and off-beat material on travel, holidays, fashion and health - is also worth trying.

With supplements, pull-outs and backgrounder specials to produce, a features editor can have more column inches to fill than a news-editor. He'll always be on the look-out for quirky items which will intrigue and amuse his readers.

Chain stores are aware of this publicity opening, sending new products to features journalists to write about. New food lines are offered for 'taste tests', cars lent for test drives, free copies of books sent for review and writers are taken on specially organised 'fact-finding' trips to factories or holiday resorts.

Even if you have a modest, locally-based, business there are still dozens of opportunities to generate 'feature copy'.

10.3 COMPETITIONS

One way of advertising 'on the cheap' is to donate products to a newspaper or radio station to be used as prizes in a readers'/listeners' competition. This guarantees that the name of your firm will be mentioned every time the competition details are given out.

Even if you represent a sports club, an amateur dramatics group or a charity you can still use this technique to gain valuable publicity. How about a first prize of a training session with your star striker, or a chance for readers to try an unusual sport like fencing or archery?

Free theatre tickets can be offered for drama fans, plus the chance to go backstage to meet the cast for drinks. Even charities can get in on the act. If you have a celebrity president why not see if he or she will be willing to be a prize for an evening - win a chance to have dinner with the star of TV's top soap!

Balloons, tee-shirts, badges and stickers are all inexpensive but make great prizes - especially for schools' painting competitions. Why not get schools to compete to design the poster to be used in your next donations campaign?

10.4 READERS' LETTERS

This section in newspapers is usually overlooked despite being an excellent platform to put across messages. Editors generally don't mind giving over space to letters from charities and community groups - even if these letters contain requests for donations. If you are letting people know that you are holding a coffee morning to raise funds, a reader's letter will do the same job as an advert - costing no more than the price of a stamp.

Letters pages are a useful publicity medium for businesses too. No editor will allow you to blatantly advertise in his letters page, but there are cunning ways to use the slot without doing a hard-sell.

If a reader's letter is published moaning about the lack of places for young people to go in the evenings, write a letter for publication replying that your go-kart track is now open and ready for customers. If another correspondent writes in to say that it's impossible to find good customer service anywhere, encourage some of your satisfied clients to drop the paper a line singing your praises.

The trick is to constantly scan the correspondence columns looking for any letter that gives you an excuse to put pen to paper. As long as you are seen to be taking part in an already open dialogue, your thinly disguised plug should be accepted.

One word of warning: the authenticity of readers' letters is thoroughly checked - so don't write in pretending to be one of your own 'satisfied customers'. You will be caught out!

10.5 SUBMITTED ARTICLES

One useful way for accountants, lawyers, financial advisers, tax specialists, DIY shops and motoring organisations to gain invaluable publicity is to offer papers or magazines free articles.

If your accountancy firm specialises in dealing with tricky tax problems, you might want to try offering your local paper an article entitled *How To Avoid The Tax Trap*. You wouldn't ask for payment. Instead all you would request is the inclusion of your photograph and a line saying what company you work for - and perhaps the address and phone number. The article would, in effect, be a huge free advertisement for your firm.

Offer your services as an expert to handle listeners' problems on local radio phone-ins. Every time the disc jockey explains who you are, your firm gets a free plug. Garden centres do particularly well this way. A member of staff will go on air to act as a 'plant doctor' to listeners with ailing blooms.

PART TWO: PAID ADVERTISING

10.6 PLAN YOUR ADVERTISING

Study your publicity needs and work out if you need to pay for advertising. Is there a particular event, new product or a slow time of the year that needs that little extra boost - a boost that editorial stories alone won't provide?

If the answer is yes, have a long think about exactly how you intend to place adverts, sketch out a rough campaign and, most importantly, estimate how much you can afford to spend.

10.7 GET ADVICE

Talk to other businesses about advertising. Find out how they approach their publicity campaigns and how much they spend. Chat to colleagues about the local media outlets they think are worth advertising with and which should be avoided.

Use any expertise they've built up over the years on the best type of advert to place and when to place it. Ring up your local paper's advertising department for advice. They can help you to work out what advertising will best suit you. This advice will be valuable, but remember it *won't* be impartial. You are dealing with salesmen and they'll be hoping to hook you.

Even if you don't advertise with them there and then, your name will go down on 'contact' lists as a possible sales lead for future advertising features. You could find yourself being regularly pestered by sales reps.

10.8 DO RESEARCH

Never advertise blind - always study the publication that you intend to advertise with and listen to any radio station that you might want to use.

See if they reflect the image you want to project. You may not want to advertise your BMW garage on a local radio station whose advertising is almost exclusively jingle-based plugs for local fast food takeaways. Neither may you want to advertise your exclusive hotel with a 'down-market' paper that specialises in sex-and-crime sensationalist reporting with huge banner headlines.

10.9 VISUALISE THE AVERAGE READER

Advertising agencies spend fortunes analysing the style and content of magazines and newspapers to find exactly the right publication in which to place their clients' adverts. They know that no two titles are the same. Each magazine fills a particular niche in the market - catering for a different segment of the population.

Agencies know who the typical buyer of any publication is and can give you a detailed run-down on the age, sex, income, social class, political views, family size and likely jobs of the target reader.

Now, you don't have the time, money or research resources of a national advertising agency but you can still do fairly accurate market research by studying the content of a newspaper or magazine in depth.

Make a note of the type of stories carried - are they designed to appeal more to men or women? Is the paper/magazine catering for working class readers or members of the professions? Does it have a strong sports section or several pages of leisure guide? Does its holiday pages cover budget weekend breaks or luxury cruises? All these are clues to the typical reader.

Look especially at the other advertisers - they've probably already done this very exercise before placing their adverts. If there are a number of businesses similar to yours or appealing to a similar type of customer to yours, then you can safely say that this publication is right for you too.

Check circulation figures

Make sure your target newspaper or radio station is the most popular in the area. There's little point advertising in a medium that isn't seen or heard by many people. Ask to be supplied with circulation/listener figures before committing yourself.

Also, check that the paper or radio station reaches *all* of the area you're targeting. Your business may be located in the fringe of a paper's circulation area so that the bulk of its readers live too far away to be interested in you.

10.10 SELECT THE MOST APPROPRIATE MEDIUM

Don't go for the grandest, most prestigious, media outlet you can find purely to enhance the image of your business. Advertising on television does give your firm a gloss of success and will impress viewers. But it will also cost you a king's ransom!

If it generates no more new business than a string of carefully placed radio and press adverts, why go to all the extra expense?

Never advertise over a larger area than necessary. There's no point promoting a window cleaning service to customers in the next county. No one will ring up and ask you to come 60 miles to clean their windows!

If you want coverage over a whole county, local radio and larger evening papers are your best bet. If you only want to speak to people in one particular town, use the local weekly newspaper.

If you just need to speak to people interested in a particular hobby or profession - a magazine or trade paper is more likely to yield results.

10.11 CHOOSE THE BEST TIME TO ADVERTISE

Pick your moment. Place your adverts at the time you're likely to reap maximum benefits. Don't advertise heavily during the summer when many people will be away on holiday and won't see their local paper or listen to their local radio. Don't advertise on Bank Holidays or just before or after Christmas or New Year - people have too much else on their plate to worry about. They won't be listening to the radio when there are Christmas specials and blockbuster films on television and parties to go to.

Be aware that newspapers attract varying numbers of readers on different days of the week. Usually, evening newspapers start off the week with few pages and get thicker as the week progresses. Friday night's paper is traditionally the thickest and best read.

Specialist supplements, printed on particular nights, can boost readership and you should be aware on what nights property sections, motoring sections and jobs sections appear. Make sensible choices - if you are offering a luxury product, it may not be worth advertising on the same night as the job section is printed. Those readers buying the paper for the situation vacant adverts probably won't have disposable income to spend on extras.

If you are trying to attract women customers find out what night the paper prints its women's page. Check to see if a paper publishes a weekend leisure guide or a 7-day TV guide on a Saturday. If not, paper sales will probably be modest as there may be little to interest readers in a thin Saturday paper.

Tie your radio advertising into popular programmes such as the morning and evening 'drive-time' programmes, quiz sections and close to any Top 20 chart rundown. These are guaranteed big audiences.

10.12 DON'T BE 'PRESSURISED' INTO ADVERTISING
Place adverts when *you* think you need them most - not when some commission-hungry advertising rep offers you a discount. It may seem like a good deal at the time, but the rep won't necessarily have your best interests at heart. He'll be more concerned with reaching sales quotas.

Don't take out an advert purely because you were rung up by a telesales rep. If reps are doing a 'ring-round' - approaching firms at random using the yellow pages as a contact source - it probably means that regular advertisers aren't taking out adverts because it's a bad time of the year for customer response.

10.13 DON'T PAY TOO MUCH
As the man with the cheque book, you have the upper hand - so always see what discounts you can negotiate.

Even if a sales department won't cut the price of your advert, they may agree to give you a larger advert for the same price, give you free 'spot colour' or a better slot, more insertions at no extra cost or offer to syndicate the advert - putting it into sister publications at a discounted rate.

Always ask for a discount if you are placing a series of adverts or are placing the same advert in several publications owned by the same company.

10.14 THINK SMALL

A full-page advert may look impressive, but it may not have much more effect than a half-page advert and is considerably dearer.

Don't make the mistake of agreeing to an advert that is much bigger than you need. Aim to create the maximum impact for the minimum amount of money. Don't opt for a grandiose display advert (an advert in a box, with large type, graphics or photos) if a small 'lineage' advert (the sort normally used for second-hand goods, lonely hearts and missing pets) would serve your purposes just as well, at a fraction of the cost.

Adverts don't have to be complicated and 'jazzy' to catch the eye. Keep it simple.

10.15 POSITION MATTERS

Don't allow your advert to be placed at random in the newspaper. Specify a good 'slot'. Make sure it appears on a well-read page. The front and back pages, sports pages, TV guide, women's page, letters page, and the 'births, deaths and marriages' page are all prime slots. You may be charged extra for having a good location, but it's worth it.

Always pick a right-hand page. They have more reader impact (that's why the Sun has its topless model on page three and not page four!) and don't allow your advert to be buried away in the middle pages of the paper. The nearer the front, the better.

10.16 ADVERTISING FEATURES

Sometimes you'll be invited to take space in a special 'theme' advert feature - Back to School, Eating Out, Quality Craftsmanship, etc. Your advert will be placed with several others - wrapped around photographs and some text. Your firm will be mentioned in the write-up, in glowing terms.

These are popular with some advertisers who think that the feature will have great impact and catch the reader's attention. Alas, this isn't necessarily true.

Readers have become wise to the wiles of advertising men and know the write-ups have been paid for and hence aren't impartial. Unfortunately, the 'editorial' section of the feature will probably have been cobbled together by a sales rep rather than being carefully written and laid-out by a journalist. The photographs may be no more than fuzzy polaroids.

It may not create the kind of impression you'd hoped for. Check that a professional journalist will be putting together the words and pictures before agreeing to buy advertising space in the feature.

10.17 SOME ADVERTISING DO'S AND DON'TS

Always:

- Make your wishes clearly known to the advertising department. If you are placing a large number of adverts, get a rep to come out and see you to discuss your needs.
- Insist on being consulted about the advert's layout and design. Don't allow an advert to be printed until you've seen and okayed the page proof.
- Insist on a second advert, printed at no cost to you, if the original is inaccurate, badly reproduced or differs from what was agreed in style, size or location.
- Check the advert after it's been printed and correct any mistakes before second or third editions of that day's paper are printed. Don't allow an incorrect advert to be used over and over without being amended.

- If you are advertising in several publications at once, ask new customers to tell you where they saw the advert. This will enable you to judge which media outlet produces the best response and allows you to target future advertising more effectively.
- Include 'feedback' devices in your advert like money-off vouchers or free tickets. If you are swamped by new customers, all clutching vouchers, you'll know the advertising was a success. If only a few vouchers are used, you'll know your advert didn't reach the target audience and you should have a rethink.

Never:
- Make exaggerated claims in your adverts. Never risk antagonising customers by making promises that you or your products can't deliver.
- Advertise on the same page as any rival business. Don't allow another firm's message to drown out your own.
- Be caught out by a huge surge of demand caused by your advert. Only seek new customers if you can cope with them.
- Have an advert that is so small that no-one notices it. It's a false economy.
- Allow a series of adverts to continue to appear if you are getting no reaction from the first ones.

One important point: advertising is an excellent way of letting people know about you and your business. But if your business is flawed and failing, no amount of advertising will save it.

CHAPTER ELEVEN

MINIMISING THE EFFECTS
OF BAD PUBLICITY

Pop stars, film moguls and professional publicists all claim there's no such thing as bad publicity. Anything that gets their name in the news and lets their public know they're still around is good 'box office'. Even negative newspaper coverage of a film can have people flocking to the cinemas to see if it's as bad as the reviewers make out.

But, you only have to look at the recently ruined careers of prominent politicians to see that bad publicity can affect lives. Lottery winners soon find their joy dented when former friends and colleagues line up to say what an undeserving rat the lucky boy really is.

While it isn't always possible to dodge negative press, you can easily avoid making things worse. A few simple steps can stop a minor crisis developing into a full-blown disaster.

11.1 PREVENTION BETTER THAN CURE

The most simple and effective way to deal with bad publicity is to avoid it in the first place. Ensure you have good press relations. Appoint a press officer and encourage him to develop links with the local press and radio and TV stations. Know who the news-editors are and be on friendly terms with them.

11.2 EXPECT THE UNEXPECTED

Don't be blind to possible media interest in your business or private life. If you are prominent in your local community, profession or sport be aware that what you say and do is newsworthy. Always think, how would this action look in print if a journalist found out?

Is anything you do likely to upset someone? If the answer is yes, then you should expect the press to be interested. Everyone is entitled to privacy, but most editors and many courts will judge public interest to outweigh an individual's right to secrecy.

Don't make the mistake of thinking that you can escape the scrutiny of the media. It's difficult to keep secrets. Even if you don't tell the local press, a disgruntled relative, colleague, neighbour or employee might. Many stories in newspapers originate from 'whistle blowers'. Perhaps the most hurtful of these are the 'kiss-and-tell' tales of former lovers.

11.3 BUILD TRUST

If a negative story does occur, the reporter will be anxious to get your side of the argument. This is where good press relations are vital.

If the reporter knows you are honest and reliable he's more likely to believe it when you tell him that the individuals complaining about you have got their facts wrong.

For example, a reporter was sent out to cover a story where a young couple claimed workmen from their local electricity board had broken into their house to disconnect the power supply, doing considerable damage to the front door and hall carpet. The couple admitted they had owed a large amount on their electricity bill over a long period of time but said they'd had no warning of the visit. There was no need for a break-in.

When the reporter contacted the electricity board to ask them about these claims, the press officer was polite, patient and helpful. He told the reporter that the couple had ignored a long string of letters - including three warning them that they would be disconnected on that date.

When the journalist went back to the couple, they admitted that what the press officer had said was true. The story was abandoned.

11.4 APPEARANCES COUNT

Always be aware of public opinion and the possible 'image' implications of all your decisions. You may be acting in good faith, doing your absolute best to be fair to your employees, colleagues, customers and local community but if your actions can be construed as dubious, underhand or callous then that's how you will be judged - no matter how wrong or damaging this is to you.

Appearances are everything. People will jump to conclusions on the sketchiest of details so be aware how you come across - especially to journalists.

11.5 WATCH YOUR TIMING

Many individuals and groups who end up with bad publicity do so not so much because of their actions but because they choose to implement these action at a bad time. It's a form of naivety not to be aware that the timing of decisions is crucial. Ask any politician - he wouldn't raise taxes just before a General Election!

As a factory manager you may have done everything in your power to avoid laying off staff. But even if you are a hero, having saved dozens of jobs, you'll be perceived as a villain if you axe some staff at Christmas. You are asking to be labelled as a Scrooge. It wouldn't cost much to wait a couple of weeks longer and avoid provoking outrage.

Some privatised utilities have had a rough ride because they've given top executives large pay rises while customer complaints have rocketed. Now, it is perfectly possible that each and every boss has earned his pay rise. But to increase charges or cut services while public opinion has been whipped up over 'fat cat salary hikes' shows naivety on a mind-boggling scale.

If you make a similar error in timing, you'll find yourself on the receiving end of bad press - and it will be *your* fault.

11.6 BE PREPARED

If a negative story blows up you must be able to quickly answer the charges, sort out any problems and ensure that the press are made aware of any mediating circumstances that will help to paint you in a better light.

To do this you need to ensure you have rapid access to necessary information and have someone used to dealing with the press to field all enquiries. A well-briefed press officer is invaluable when things go wrong and you are bombarded with reporters' questions.

11.7 YOU MUST ACT

Don't allow a minor problem to escalate. One bad story is unfortunate, but a series of bad stories can be disastrous. Coverage criticising you will be seen by others who may also feel aggrieved. They'll add their voices to the clamour of disquiet - leading to more stories, and more people with complaints coming forward.

Don't try to ride out the storm. The bad publicity won't magically go away. It will whip up into a typhoon. Take positive steps to end the negative coverage. Apologise for mistakes, be seen to be putting things right and co-operate fully with reporters.

Hoover must kick themselves for not dealing more swiftly and professionally with the wave of complaints that arose from their free flights promotion. The trouble sprang from a genuine mistake - the company's surprise that so many people would take up the airline tickets offer - but by the time managers had allowed negative coverage to go on for weeks, there were suggestions that Hoover hadn't played fair by its customers and the company's image had been badly tarnished.

The Hoover case is a useful example. If you allow a series of negative stories to be printed over a period of time, you will not only suffer from news stories but you'll also attract the attention of magazines, trade papers, newspaper features departments and TV consumer programmes.

A good rule of thumb is: don't allow a problem to continue long enough for a newspaper or TV station to have their artists compile special graphics and logos. These visual devices are extremely damaging - helping to burn a company's name in the public's consciousness for all the wrong reasons.

11.8 DON'T STALL OR BE AWKWARD
Although it is legitimate to demand time to properly deal with any accusations, it isn't a good idea to stall in the vain hope that everything will just blow over.

It's no use refusing to return calls or saying that there is no-one authorised to talk to the press or that your press officer is away on holiday. It won't stop the story running and you'll have lost the opportunity to put right any wrong facts.

11.9 DON'T LIE
Having found yourself on the receiving end of bad publicity don't make things worse by trying to lie your way out of trouble or instigate a cover-up. If you're caught - and most people are - you'll be seen as being dishonest and nothing you say will be believed. You may be innocent of the original charges but the botched cover-up will mean no-one will give you the benefit of the doubt.

11.10 DON'T CLAM UP
Beware falling into the trap of saying 'no comment' when approached by a reporter. Through repeated overuse this

phrase has taken on unfortunate connotations. When a reader sees this he'll assume that you are staying quiet because you are guilty and therefore afraid to talk.

It's even crept into TV. Watch any police drama and see how often criminals say 'no comment" when the police interrogate them. The louder they say it, the more guilty they appear to viewers. It's far better to say something bland and inoffensive than to refuse to speak.

11.11 CONTROL RUMOURS
Many negative stories occur because rumours spring up where there is a lack of hard, checkable, facts. When approached by a reporter, honesty can often be the best policy. It may be that by revealing a few extra details about your planning application or staff restructuring you can allay the fears of those affected and hence immediately neutralise the bad press.

11.12 SPEAK 'OFF THE RECORD'
Most reporters are happy for you to speak to them 'off the record' if it frees you to be able to explain to them why the story they have is inaccurate or misleading. A good reporter is more interested in getting the facts right than in pillorying anyone.

If you feel there is 'more than meets the eye' about a complaint against you, tell the reporter in confidence. The reporter won't be happy about being used as a weapon against you, and will welcome any extra information you can supply about the person stirring up the story.

This is not a get-out clause where you can sling mud back in an attempt to deflect blame, but it is a useful device for ensuring there is no miscarriage of justice.

It all depends on trust. Only go 'off the record' with a reporter you know well. You have no legal recourse against a reporter who uses 'off-record' material without permission.

Be aware that trust runs both ways. A reporter may be unwilling to let you go off the record if he thinks you're using the device to wriggle out of giving a proper interview.

To avoid any confusion, start the private part of the conversation with: *"I'm talking off the record. I don't want to be quoted on this."* When you are happy to be quoted say: *"Going back on the record, what I'm prepared to say is ...."*

11.13 DON'T BULLY

Many company bosses try to rant and bluster their way out of trouble. When a reporter rings up, some managing directors make loud, angry, threats - usually to sue the paper involved.

It never works. It normally achieves the opposite effect - alienating the reporter and convincing him that there must be something in the story. After all, a journalist thinks, why try to frighten off a reporter unless you've got something to hide?

The worst possible thing to do is try to name-drop or pull strings. The moment a reporter hears the words: *"I happen to play golf with your publisher"* or *"I advertise with your radio station and I'll withdraw all my ads"* he'll make sure your negative story is given lead story status - just to prove he can't be got at.

11.14 DON'T BE BULLIED

Although you should co-operate with the media, don't allow yourself to be tricked or manipulated into saying something you'll regret.

Some reporters have the annoying habit of spending hours researching a 'knocking' story then ringing up the person who is the subject of the allegations with only half an hour or so to go to deadline. They pressurise the interviewee by saying: *"My copy is about to go to the sub-editors and you'd better say something to me just now or it'll go into print without your side of the story."*

Don't allow this to happen to you. Don't let the journalist bully you into making an ill-advised off-the-cuff statement. Insist on having adequate time to reply in detail - when you've had a chance to investigate the allegations fully. Your statement that: *"Sorry I don't know anything about this"* can be used in such a context that it appears that you're actually saying *"... and I don't care."*

A journalist has a **duty** under the National Union of Journalists' code of conduct to present stories that are fair, accurate and balanced. If the person attacking you has had time to present a 'prosecution' case, then it's only fair that you be given a reasonable amount of time to prepare a 'defence' case.

Point out to the reporter that you are anxious to help but are equally as anxious to supply him with accurate information. Suggest that as you can't do this in half-an-hour he would be advised to consider delaying the publication of the story until it is available - perhaps later that day or early next morning.

11.15 IF HE REFUSES

If the journalist tells you that he can't delay the story, don't worry. Simply give him the quote: *"I am sorry to hear that there are allegations against me/my firm/my club. Naturally, I will look into these as a matter of urgency and issue a full statement when I have learnt the facts."* Say no more than that.

This quote should be sufficient to act as a 'holding action' without giving anything away. You haven't accepted blame for anything, nor have you seemed cavalier or uncaring.

Tell the reporter you expect this quote to be used in full. Insist that any further statement from you that day is used - again, in full - in any subsequent editions or bulletins.

Although there is no guarantee, the thought of having to continually update a story during the day may convince an overworked reporter that it's worth holding off for a day until you issue a 'definitive' reply.

11.16 HOLD ON TO THE INITIATIVE

Just because a reporter rang you, it doesn't mean you have to deal over the phone. Tell him, politely, that you'll be delighted to talk to him about the story - but only face to face.

As well as ensuring that you aren't answering a disembodied accuser, it may also delay the story's publication. It may well be that the reporter can't come to see you until after all the editions of that day's paper have been printed.

This is particularly important when dealing with regional television reporters. Remember, a local TV reporter will have to go back to the studio - probably quite some distance away - and edit the piece. After 4 pm it becomes a struggle for a reporter to get a story ready to put on air in the main tea-time programme. If it misses this programme, the story is likely to be shelved until the next morning.

11.17 KNOW WHAT YOU ARE BEING ACCUSED OF

Don't settle for a reporter's glib summary of the allegations. Insist on having them put to you in detail. If there are documents, ask to see them.

Insist on the reporter naming the people who are making the allegations. The accused has a right to know his accusers. Don't be flannelled by a reporter who says: *"We've received lots of complaints about you."*

Demand he tell you how many complaints, what they claim and who exactly has complained. It is an old reporter's trick to write: *"Neighbours were up in arms"* when only one neighbour has a grouse - and that complaint doesn't bear careful scrutiny.

11.18 DEMAND FAIR TREATMENT

Point out that you expect to be given adequate space to refute any allegations - a roughly equivalent space to put your side of the story.

Tell him that you expect your denial to be prominently positioned in the story - within the first three sentences - not tagged on to the end of the copy as an afterthought. Also tell him that you expect the denial 'angle' to feature in any headline - people are influenced by headlines. They help to shape reader opinion.

As the headline is written by a sub-editor back in the office, the reporter in question won't be able to promise this. That doesn't matter. What does matter is that you will have put over the message that you will scrutinise *every* aspect of the story that is printed ... and so will your lawyer!

11.19 AVOID INTERVIEWS

If the negative story about you *is* accurate and correct, there's no point making things worse by giving those attacking you more ammunition. Limit the quotes and facts you give out to the media.

The best damage limitation method is to refuse all interviews but issue a short, factual, written statement. Insist that it is used in full, in context.

Set out whatever defence you can and leave it at that. Do not offer any additional information. Answering reporter's 'follow-up' questions will only allow the press to re-open the debate and give you the opportunity to put your foot in it.

11.20 USE THE OPPORTUNITY

Any clever businessman will tell you that a customer complaint doesn't necessarily have to be a disaster - it can be an opportunity. If you can show concern and act swiftly to put right any problem you can not only win back that customer's loyalty but make him feel even better about you than he did in the first place.

The same principle holds true in publicity terms. You can turn a small problem into a public relations triumph by being seen to care about people and seen to be doing your best to make amends. You can show your club or business has sense of civic duty and moral responsibility.

Bad publicity needn't be the end of the world - as long as you act professionally. For example, a small factory accidentally allowed waste overflow to seep into a nearby river, killing large numbers of fish. The firm, anxious to put right this environmental damage (and aware of the public relations implications) paid to have the river cleaned and restocked.

By ensuring that the clean-up operation received the same amount of coverage as the spillage, the firm avoided a major uproar from the local community. The press and TV coverage of local school-children helping the firm's workmen to release the new fish was so positive that some reports failed to mention that the firm was responsible for the pollution in the first place!

Dealing with bad publicity is a real test of character. Always stay cool, and in control. Most people in the spotlight have to endure bad press some time in their lives. The trick is not to take it personally. Grace under fire is a necessary public relations skill.

CHAPTER TWELVE

POTENTIAL PITFALLS

Cynics will tell you that dealing with the press is a minefield - one wrong step and *'Boom'*, a story blows up in your face.

While not subscribing to this view most journalists would admit that when you invite the press into your home, club or business you sometimes run the risk of opening a proverbial Pandora's Box. You never quite know what you are unleashing. So it's a wise idea to consider first whether you have anything in your life that you'd rather have kept quiet.

It needn't be as dramatic as a well hidden criminal record or a string of mistresses. A vocal relative with a grudge or a disgruntled partner from a failed business venture are enough to spoil even the best organised publicity campaign.

12.1 NO CONTROL

Once you've contacted a newspaper or TV company you have little or no say over how your story is covered. Unlike advertising space - where you pay for the privilege of saying whatever you like about your product or company, no matter how biased or positively-angled - editorial space is deemed to be neutral, free of undue advertisers' influences. Reporters are free to write what they like, as long as they don't defame you or knowingly print lies.

This means you have no control over how a finished story looks, what impression it gives or what angle the writer might take. You can request to see the proposed story before it is printed, but most editors will refuse - seeing this as a slur on the accuracy and professionalism of their staff.

12.2 WRONG ANGLE

News editors may take only a small section of your press release - the part you think least interesting - and ditch the rest. They may take the information and use in it in a way you hadn't even considered.

For example, your Sunday League football team is delighted to have won three important games in a row, scoring twelve breath-taking goals. ***United Dish Up A Goals Feast*** is the headline you are expecting.

However, the news editor or sports editor may be more interested in the fact that you've won three games after a long run of defeats. The headline becomes ***Battered United End Goals Famine*** - not nearly as positive.

Alternatively, your company may be delighted that 30 per cent of potential customers in your town buy your new product. The paper may choose to go on the angle that 70 per cent of your potential customers ***don't*** buy it.

12.3 ROVING REPORTER

Having invited a reporter into your factory or home, he may witness things you didn't want him to see. He may have arrived to report on the new packaging machine you've installed, but if the reporter has to pass workers picketing about the rise in canteen prices he's bound to be intrigued about the dispute.

Likewise, if you hold a press conference to announce your sports club's new star signing don't be surprised if reporters see this an excuse to quiz you on the club's poor performance or disciplinary record.

12.4 BEING MISQUOTED

There is nothing so irritating and potentially damaging than being misquoted or misrepresented. Even if you immediately ring up the editor and demand a correction/apology there may be a delay before it appears. The correction may not be seen by the same readers who saw the original incorrect story. Evening paper readers, especially, tend only to buy those issues which contain a major feature of interest to them - car sections, property ads, situation vacant pull-outs. A reader may see the misleading article about you in the Monday issue but not buy the Tuesday issue containing the corrected version.

It's difficult to completely prevent yourself from being misquoted, but you can take steps to lessen the risk. Only deal with a journalist you know and trust. Only deal face to face - it's easy to get things wrong over a telephone. Tape the interview using a small, portable tape recorder, having first informed the journalist that you intend doing this.

Not only will this give you 'evidence' to present to the editor, but it will impress upon the reporter that you won't tolerate any inaccuracies. If the reporter refuses to co-operate with this, do not allow the interview to go ahead.

12.5 COMPLAINING

If you do feel you've been badly treated, don't allow yourself to be fobbed off with excuses by the newsdesk or the reporter involved. Insist on dealing with the editor. If he refuses to take your complaint seriously, a short sharp solicitor's letter will convince him of your sincerity. Usually that is enough to get his attention.

Be especially wary of any offer from a reporter to do a second story 'to put the record straight'. This probably means that no-one at the paper has spotted the mistake and the reporter is hoping to mollify you while keeping out of trouble.

If you agree to a second story, you allow the reporter to go on misquoting others and to do this without his bosses knowing there's a problem. You also run the very real risk of being misquoted or misrepresented again because the original incorrect story will be placed in the paper's cuttings library and will be used as a reference source by other reporters doing stories on you. If you complain, at the very least, the library copy of the story will be amended.

Remember: no matter how angry you feel always be calm, reasonable and non-threatening when you complain. Most editors will be genuinely horrified to find out about your problem and will do their best to rectify mistakes.

12.6 CHANGING YOUR MIND
There's a huge psychological difference between making an off-the-cuff comment in conversation and seeing it recorded for posterity. You may find that the statement you've made takes on a whole new and worrying significance when it appears in black and white. Even quite mild rebukes can seem to be damning attacks when printed. Humorous remarks, especially, can be offensive if treated as serious or seen 'out of context.'

If you think there is even the remotest chance that you'll regret what you've said or will want to change your mind, don't allow yourself to be quoted. Once it has appeared, you can't take it back.

12.7 BLAST FROM THE PAST
Badly thought-out statements have a habit of hanging around to haunt you for years afterwards. Just think of the teacher who told Einstein that he'd amount to nothing!

Reporters delve back into old stories for background and old quotes you made in haste or anger can be exhumed and reprinted time and time again - causing you maximum embarrassment.

Politicians, even local politicians, are always being hit over the head with former statements - usually showing they've done a 'U-turn'. Circumstances change and so do opinions - we all adapt our feelings - but if you are demonstrated to have held one view ten years ago and now hold a contrary viewpoint, you may be seen by critics as dishonest, opportunist or just plain fickle.

Journalists like nothing better than exposing hypocrisy and humbug, so be extremely careful what you say when interviewed. Don't make promises in print that you can't deliver or may later want to go back on. One day, long in the future, you may be hanged with your own words.

12.8 DID I REALLY WEAR THAT?

Photographs and filmed interviews are kept on library file - sometimes for decades. If a newspaper or TV station wants a picture to illustrate a story involving you they may decide it is cheaper and quicker to dig out an old still from the library, rather than arrange to have an up-to-date picture taken.

Now this may not be a problem. But if the picture the paper has shows you years ago as a long-haired hippy in '70s flares and velvet jacket and you are now the local bank manager, you may quite rightly feel that the old print is both misleading and embarrassing.

You may request that a news organisation doesn't use an old or unflattering picture of you but you can't demand that they stop. One way to get round this is to ensure that all news releases or handouts sent out by you have a flattering, up-to-date photograph attached.

12.9 LABELLING

Journalists like to be able to put labels on people as an easy shorthand way of describing them to readers. This may be fine if you are a successful businessman and are constantly referred to in print as a 'top boss' or 'leading entrepreneur'. But it becomes less flattering if you were once a bankrupt or the organiser of an unsuccessful event.

Even though that episode of your life has long passed, reporters - consulting old cuttings - will refer to you as 'former bankrupt' or 'architect of the flop Expo 92 exhibition' even though it has no direct bearing on the current story.

The new council-run swimming pool in one town had a few teething problems with cracked tiles but the local paper insisted on describing it as the 'crisis-hit leisure centre' years after the problems had been solved.

Labelling is particularly irksome to actors. Martin Shaw, for instance, played the role of CI5's Ray Doyle more than two decades ago. Yet newspapers still refer to him as the former Professionals star. He may quite rightly wonder what he has to do in 20 years to earn a more up-to-date label.

12.10 JEALOUSY
Blowing your own trumpet

You only have to look at the scores of 'hate' stories that appear in the national press about big jackpot lottery winners, and see how many people take delight in reading them, to know that jealousy is a powerful emotion.

If you trumpet your successes over the pages of your local paper not everyone will necessarily share your joy or wish you well. Even within your own sport or business rivals may see your publicity as boasting or putting on airs and graces. The very British idea of being modest at all times, can be offended by a banner headline declaring that you've out-competed, out-sold, out-smarted the rest.

If even a small story about your triumphs is going to cause disharmony, antagonise partners or jeopardise already fragile business relationships, you may decide that it's better to skip the media coverage in exchange for a quieter or less hassled life.

No one is safe from the green-eyed monster
Even within a small local club rivalries can fester. If you are the press officer and often have your name in print, or are the type of person who gives reporters the kind of 'lively, controversial' quotes they seek you will probably annoy someone close by.

Take the unhappy individual to one side and explain that the coverage is good for all of you in the club. If this still doesn't end his or her jealousy, suggest that a different club member be appointed as press officer each year. This has the spin-off benefit of providing the club, over time, with several individuals who understand the do's and don'ts of dealing with the media.

12.11 LOSING CREDIBILITY
It's common for doctors, lawyers and accountants who are often quoted in print to end up on the receiving end of their colleague's censure or derision. *"What makes you think you're so special?"* or *"Who said you could act as a spokesman for the profession?"* are frequent reactions.

Professionals who do radio show phone-ins or who have their name and picture printed above newspaper advice columns are often accused of 'entering showbiz' or 'hogging the limelight'. Always beware that acting as a pundit, agony aunt or a 'rent-a-quote' regular can harm your professional reputation or credibility. It's a trap that many MPs have fallen into.

12.12 INVASION OF PRIVACY
Once you seek publicity, you effectively give away the right to total privacy. Even if you only want your business to be featured, you run the risk of shining a light in all corners of your life. Without you realising it, your drink-drive conviction could become a story. So could the long-running feud with your neighbours over the boundary fence.

Showbiz personalities who have become estranged from close family members, often fall victim to stories about their 'insensitivity' or 'meanness.' *Brother Lived In Poverty While Star Lived The High Life*.

12.13 UNWANTED ATTENTION

Reporters looking into secret parts of your life may not be the only unwelcome attention you attract. While it is still comparatively rare for 'unbalanced' or 'dangerous' characters to pester you because you've appeared in a newspaper, thieves can and do look through publications where unwitting interviewees pose self-consciously beside their prized antiques, cars or expensively furnished homes.

While most editors are responsible people, who wouldn't knowingly print information that helps burglars, it does sometimes happen. The best defence you have is to ask the paper to be vague about such details as your exact address or the value of prized items being mentioned.

12.14 BEING SEEN AS A SOFT TOUCH

Thieves aren't the only people who go through newspapers looking for targets. Life Assurance salesmen and other marketing teams scour news and feature pages for likely clients. So don't be surprised to receive a phone call from a stranger saying: *"I saw the Gazette story about you winning the £2,000 prize as manager of the month and I thought to myself - I wonder if he knows the wonderful benefits of our pension plan/ double glazing/ dance aerobics course?"*

Stories which make you appear affluent can attract begging letters and approaches from groups seeking sponsorship/ donated prizes/ grants or plain old-fashioned handouts. If you are a soft touch who can't turn down such requests, it might be worth considering the cost of this before appearing in print.

12.15 BIG BROTHER

Even the Government uses the surveillance ploy of scanning papers and broadcast news reports. Several civil service agencies monitor newspapers for details on potential fraudsters/ tax evaders/ dole scroungers/ absentee fathers etc.

A few years ago an evening newspaper interviewed a deep sea diver working on oil rigs in the North Sea. When asked by the reporter how much he earned, he was a little cagey about giving an exact figure but said with a wink: *"Just put it that I'm not exactly starving"!*

The day after the feature article was printed, he received a phone call from the Inland Revenue. Now, you may think that kind of tactic is unfair and tantamount to snooping, but it does go on and you may not want to unwittingly add to a bulging manila folder sitting in some Government office.

12.16 BECOMING A PROTEST TARGET

There now exist a bewildering assortment of professional protesters and 'Eco-warriors' who are willing to take what they call direct action against people and companies they see as being immoral.

Beware of attracting their attention if you are involved in any way with live animal exports, experiments on animals, road building, the fur trade, the meat trade, arms manufacture, working with mahogany or any other 'threatened' Rain Forest wood, building on disputed nature sites or are the landlord of empty properties. Publicity, even positive publicity, will make you more likely to be a target.

12.17 CUTTINGS SERVICES

You may wrongly assume that having local publicity is okay because your estranged wife/ former business partners/ creditors/ unwanted fans or scrounging relatives live in another part of the country and hence won't see the stories.

Newspapers and video tapes find their way around the country and abroad - people post them to their relatives or to friends who've moved away but who still have an affection and interest in their old home town. This means you can't say for sure just who will see your story or where they'll be.

This problem is exacerbated by the existence of cuttings services whose only job is to search all Britain's publications looking for mentions of various people, products or firms. If one of their clients is someone you'd rather avoid, it makes no difference that your story appeared in the South and that the person chasing you lives in the far North. They *will* find out.

All this may sound a bit disturbing, but problems resulting from newspaper stories are usually the exception rather than the rule. Potential pitfalls can easily be avoided with a little foresight. Always try to be aware of any possible negative consequences of the publicity you seek. If you have worries, discuss these with the editor of the newspaper involved. You'll find that, in most cases, that journalists are both reasonable and sympathetic.

CHAPTER THIRTEEN

CASE STUDIES

It's difficult to predict with certainty how well any publicity campaign will go. There are so many different factors that can affect the outcome - did your event clash with a larger, rival, attraction? Did you contact the right newspapers and radio stations at just the right moment? Did you make an effective sales pitch? Were the news-editors short of stories? Were you ready to handle the flood of press enquiries your press releases generated?

If you've followed all the media advice in this book, you will have maximised your chances of hitting the headlines. You've targeted your publicity as accurately as possible, found the angle that captures the imagination and presented your news in a punchy, attention-grabbing format. But have you done as well as you should have? Have you gained as much coverage as you'd planned?

This concluding chapter contains three case studies based on the experiences of different groups who set out to gain as much media coverage as possible. See how well their media campaigns went compared to yours. You may find some interesting lessons from their successes and the snags they encountered.

CASE STUDY 1: THE PIZZA PARLOUR

Gerry O'Neil knew what he wanted to do with his redundancy money - open a small pizzeria. With a flair for cooking and an Italian wife, Gerry was convinced he could make a success in the fast food business. The bank was sympathetic but, even with a sizeable loan, the only site Gerry could afford was in the back streets of Dunston town centre.

Previously, it had been a video rental shop which had gone bust but Gerry was confident his pizza parlour would make a good profit. It was near bedsit land where hundreds of students from the local college lived and a couple of streets away from a shoe factory which stayed open all round the clock. The factory's canteen was only open between 8 am and 4 pm so Gerry had high hopes of supplying a stream of takeaway pizzas to hungry night-shift workers.

THE PROBLEM

By the time Gerry opened he'd used up nearly all his cash - there was nothing left to pay for advertising. He did attract some customers - many curious to see "what the new place was like" but not enough to cover the overheads. It seemed to take a long time for word to spread around the students and the factory workers lost interest when Gerry told them he couldn't deliver pizzas - he couldn't leave the restaurant unattended and the shoe workers were reluctant to come out to collect them.

"It looked as though I was on the fast track to bankruptcy," Gerry said. *"I needed advertising to let people know we existed*

*but I couldn't afford advertising without selling a hell of a lot
more pizzas. It was a classic Catch 22."*

THE SOLUTION

A friend who worked in PR advised Gerry to contact his local
commercial radio station and pitch them 'a deal'. If the disc
jockeys would plug the restaurant, he'd give several free meals
as competition prizes. He'd also give half price pizzas to anyone
coming into the pizzeria and reciting any of the station's jingles.
The station jumped at the idea - especially when Gerry invited
the staff down for a free sample. Before the week was through
the restaurant was being mentioned on the air ten times a day.

THE AFTERMATH

The campaign ran for a month and a half. Business at the pizza
parlour more than trebled, and Gerry was able to take on
someone to do deliveries.

*"Some customers only came in to take advantage of the
money off offer and we never saw them again,"* Gerry said, *"but
we did hang on to a fair number of regulars and they kept us
afloat until we became established."* Since then Gerry has done
two more promotions with the radio station and a highly
successful cheap pizza voucher offer in the local weekly paper.

"Without publicity we'd have gone to the wall for sure," he
said. *"I've told my friend that he single-handedly saved us. It
was a brilliant idea to contact the radio station. I've told him he's
on free meals for life!"*

CASE STUDY 2: THE CHARITY BRANCH

The Dunston Branch of the Stroke Recovery Trust decided that
it was time they attracted more members and more funds to
help stroke sufferers. They approached local journalist, Lucy
Mitchells - whose father was recovering from a stroke - to ask if
she would act as their press officer.

*"I said yes at once, thinking it would be easy as I already
worked on the local TV station and knew most of the area's
news-editors,"* Lucy said, *"but I found that as soon as I looked*

into the best ways of raising the Trust's profile it proved to be a much bigger job than I'd imagined. I thought I'd knock out a few quick press releases and fix up the occasional photograph but for a year it took up nearly every spare moment I had."

THE PROBLEM
Although the Trust had some good local press links with weekly newspapers, it wasn't getting more than a few lines in print. Larger newspapers, the local radio stations and the TV company didn't give any coverage at all. Journalists didn't think the Trust's work would interest their readers, listeners or viewers.

"No-one actually yawned when I talked to them about the Trust but I could tell we just weren't exciting enough to warrant decent media coverage," Lucy said. *"even people in my own newsroom told me to forget it. Stroke victims don't make good TV pictures."*

THE SOLUTION
Lucy looked back through the news items that the Trust had been sending in prior to appointing her as press officer. Although there was basically nothing wrong with the material from a journalistic viewpoint, it suffered from being written in a dull, matter-of-fact way; dealing almost exclusively with small-scale events like flag days, annual general meetings and appeals for support by the branch chairman.

"I decided that we were going to throw away the stale, lifeless 'committee reports' approach and find real live news stories - stories involving individual members of the branch - human stories that readers would relate to."

Lucy decided on one major publicity thrust to put the Trust into the headlines - a high profile fund-raising event with an unusual angle and plenty of photo opportunities.

The fund-raiser turned out to be comparatively easy to set up. Jack, the branch chairman, had been a fireman before his stroke, and had kept in touch with his former colleagues.

They readily agreed to help out - suggesting a tug of war contest with a difference. Why not get teams of firemen to compete against each other to see who could tow a fire engine, tied to a length of rope, the furthest. Jack could sit at the wheel of the fire engine - great for pictures.

"I knew it was a winner as soon as I heard," Lucy said, *"I had no trouble getting all the coverage we wanted. Everyone was interested - we had preview stories, reporters and photographers turning up on the day and later we had several shorter items saying how much the event had raised."*

Because the fire-engine pull was on a quiet newsday, the event even attracted a TV film crew. A short report went out on that evening's local news programme.

THE AFTERMATH

Having convinced news-editors that the Trust's work could generate good news stories, Lucy followed up the success of the fund-raiser with an awareness week.

The week, which took three months of planning and organisation, featured exhibitions, talks to community groups, full-page feature articles in the local evening paper,   radio phone-ins and two personality pieces which were broadcast on TV on consecutive nights. *"I prepared a detailed press pack on the work of the Trust, how strokes affect people's lives and the need for more resources and understanding,"* Lucy said. *"As well as press releases on various events we were running, I interviewed three stroke sufferers and their families and put together human-interest stories which could be used word for word."*

The awareness week was so successful that other branches - seeing all the publicity - thought it was a national campaign and phoned up the Trust's head office angrily demanding to know why they hadn't been told about it! Dunston branch's membership almost doubled in one year and donations soared.

"I'm not saying that I did anything that any of the other branch members couldn't have," Lucy said, *"but I feel it helped enormously to see things through a journalist's eyes. The Trust*

had dozens of great stories to tell but they couldn't identify what would interest the media. It took a professional to sell them as a fascinating group well worthy of column inches."

CASE STUDY 3: THE AMATEUR DRAMATICS GROUP

The Stapleford Players had never needed more than the occasional news item in the local press. As a well-known and popular amateur dramatics group, the Players attracted reasonable sized audiences to their twice yearly productions.

"Apart from the odd line in the local evening newspaper we received all the publicity we needed through word of mouth," club president Brenda Hedges said, *"we had lots of friends and supporters and people always seemed to know what show we were presenting next and most tickets were sold well in advance."*

The group were lucky in having a local building society manageress amongst their members and were given the use of a window in the high street branch. The window display, including photographs of previous shows, always caught the eye of shoppers.

THE PROBLEM

It became apparent to Brenda and the others that they didn't have enough men in the group. The Players had attracted less men each year until there were only two left.

It wasn't just that the lack of males was restricting the choice of shows the Players could tackle, but the group didn't have enough strong arms to move scenery and props around.

"We soldiered on for a year or so but it became obvious that things couldn't go on the way they were," Brenda said. *"Tempers got frayed and several members said that if we didn't attract some more men - and quickly - they'd leave."*

THE SOLUTION

"I'd have preferred to approach the local paper casually and get the editor to put in a few paragraphs appealing for some men to help out," Brenda said, *" but I felt circumstances were so bad that we needed a little drama and urgency to get the message across."*

Ringing up, Brenda was put straight on to a reporter when she told the newsdesk that the Players faced a "disaster." *"I probably went a little over the top,"* Brenda admitted, *"but it did the trick. The paper printed a big story saying that we'd fold for sure if we didn't have some male volunteers come to our rescue."*

Five men did join the Players as a result of the story - **Players Face The Final Curtain** - but the story created a little more drama than Brenda had anticipated.

THE AFTERMATH

She was contacted by several loyal supporters who'd got the wrong end of the stick and believed the club had folded.

*"I had to explain that I hadn't said that we **would** fold but that we **might** fold. Some people understood that it was only a ploy to generate publicity but others seemed totally baffled by the whole episode."*

The confusion continued when Brenda was asked by the local radio station if they could interview her about the fact that the club had been disbanded then miraculously relaunched - they'd got the story third-hand (and inaccurately) from a local freelance journalist who'd overheard two people talking about it in the pub!

Advance ticket sales for the Player's next show were abysmal - fans assumed the Players had given up - and ironically Brenda had to beg a second story in the evening paper to give the show a desperately needed plug. Unfortunately, from that day on the paper described the Players *as a group - "snatched from the jaws of disaster."*

"It's my own fault," Brenda said, *"I should have been honest from the start and not tried to fool anyone but I had no idea how*

it would all snowball. You may find it strange but even now I'm not against publicity - I still talk to all the local press - but I think more about what I say and the impact it will have."

CONCLUSION

Any of these three experiences ring a bell? Has anything similar happened to you or someone you know?

Dealing with the press can seem daunting but it needn't be a nightmare as Gerry and Lucy's stories illustrate. Even Brenda admits the problems that followed her melodramatic announcement were mostly of her own making.

If you are straight with the media and know how publicity works, you should have a long, fruitful and happy relationship with your local news outfits.

I hope this book has helped you see new opportunities to promote yourself, your business or your group. No matter what your circumstances or where you are based, the publicity principles we've covered should make you more confident, knowledgeable and professional about approaching the press.

So what are you waiting for? Don't hold back any longer - pick up the phone or write that press release. Isn't it time you were **Hitting The Headlines**?

USEFUL ADDRESSES AND PHONE NUMBERS

NATIONAL NEWSPAPERS

DAILY EXPRESS
Ludgate House, 245 Blackfriars Road, London SE1 9UX
Tel: 0171 928 8000

DAILY MAIL
Northcliffe House, 2 Derry Street, Kensington, London W8 5TT
Tel: 0171 938 6000

DAILY MIRROR
1 Canada Square, Canary Wharf, London E14 5AP
Tel: O171 293 3000

DAILY SPORT
19 Great Ancoats Street, Manchester M60 4BT
Tel: 0161 236 4466

DAILY STAR
Ludgate House, 245 Blackfriars Road, London SE1 9UX
Tel: 0171 928 8000

THE DAILY TELEGRAPH
1 Canada Square, Canary Wharf, London E14 5DT
Tel: 0171 538 5000

FINANCIAL TIMES
1 Southwark Bridge, London SE1 9HL
Tel: 0171 873 3000

THE GUARDIAN
119 Farringdon Road, London EC1R 3ER
Tel: 0171 278 2332

THE INDEPENDENT
1 Canada Square, Canary Wharf, London E14 5AP.
Tel: 0171 293 2000

MORNING STAR
1-3 Ardleigh Road, London N1 4HS
Tel: 0171 254 0033

THE SUN
1 Virginia Street, Wapping, London E1 9XP
Tel: 0171 782 4000

THE TIMES
1 Pennington Street, London E1 9XN
Tel: 0171 782 5000

SUNDAYS
INDEPENDENT ON SUNDAY
1 Canada Square, Canary Wharf, London E14 5AP
Tel: 0171 293 2000

THE MAIL ON SUNDAY
Northcliffe House, 2 Derry Street, Kensington, London W8 5TS
Tel: 0171 938 6000

THE NEWS OF THE WORLD
1 Virginia Street, Wapping, London E1 9XR
Tel: 0171 782 4000

THE OBSERVER
119 Farringdon Road, London EC1R 3ER
Tel: 0171 278 2332

THE PEOPLE
1 Canada Square, Canary Wharf, London E14 5AP
Tel: 0171 293 3000

SUNDAY EXPRESS
Ludgate House, 245 Blackfriars Road, London SE1 9UX
Tel: 0171 928 8000

SUNDAY MIRROR
1 Canada Square, Canary Wharf, London E14 5AP
Tel: 0171 293 3000

SUNDAY SPORT
19 Great Ancoats Street, Manchester M60 4BT
Tel: 0161 236 4466

SUNDAY TELEGRAPH
1 Canada Square, Canary Wharf, London E14 5DT
Tel: 0171 538 5000

THE SUNDAY TIMES
1 Pennington Street, London E1 9XW
Tel: 0171 782 5000

SCOTLAND
DAILY RECORD
Anderston Quay, Glasgow G3 8DA
Tel: 0141 248 7000

GLASGOW HERALD
195 Albion Street, Glasgow G1 1QP
Tel: 0141 552 6255

THE SCOTSMAN
20 North Bridge, Edinburgh EH1 1YT
Tel: 0131 225 2468

SCOTLAND ON SUNDAY
20 North Bridge, Edinburgh EH1 1YT
Tel: 0131 225 2468

SUNDAY MAIL
Anderston Quay, Glasgow G3 8DA
Tel: 0141 248 7000

SUNDAY POST
2 Albert Square, Dundee DD1 9QJ
Tel: 01382 223131

WALES
WALES ON SUNDAY
Thomson House, Havelock Street, Cardiff CF1 1WR
Tel: 01222 223333

NORTHERN IRELAND
SUNDAY LIFE
124-144 Royal Avenue, Belfast BT1 1EB
Tel: 01232 331133

TELEVISION
BBC NEWS AND CURRENT AFFAIRS
Television Centre, Wood Lane, London W12 7RJ
Tel: 0181 743 8000

BBC MIDLANDS AND EAST
Broadcasting Centre, Pebble Mill Road, Birmingham B5 7QQ
Tel: 0121 414 8888

Nottingham
East Midlands Broadcasting Centre, York House, Mansfield
Road, Nottingham NG1 3JB
Tel: 0115 9472395

Norwich
St Catherine's Close, All Saint's Green, Norwich NR1 3ND
Tel: 01603 619331

BBC NORTH
New Broadcasting House, Oxford Road, Manchester M60 1SJ
Tel: 0161 200 2020

Leeds
Broadcasting Centre, Woodhouse Lane, Leeds LS2 9PX
Tel: 01132 441188

Newcastle upon Tyne
Broadcasting Centre, Barrack Road, Newcastle NE99 2NE
Tel: 0191 232 1313

BBC SOUTH
Broadcasting House, Whiteladies Road, Bristol BS8 2LR
Tel: 0117 9732211

Bristol (As above)

Southampton
Broadcasting House, Havelock Road, Southampton SO1 1XQ
Tel: 01703 226201

Plymouth
Broadcasting House, Seymour Road, Plymouth PL3 5BD
Tel: 01752 229201

BBC SOUTH EAST
Elstree Centre, Clarendon Road, Borehamwood WD6 1JF
Tel: 0181 953 6100

BBC SCOTLAND
Broadcasting House, Queen Margaret Drive, Glasgow G12 8DG
Tel: 0141 330 8844

Aberdeen
Broadcasting House, Beechgrove Terrace, Aberdeen AB9 2ZT
Tel: 01224 625233

Dundee
Nethergate Centre, 66 Nethergate, Dundee DD1 4ER
Tel: 01382 202481

Edinburgh
Broadcasting House, Queen Street, Edinburgh EH2 1JF
Tel: 0131 469 4200

Inverness
7 Culduthel Road, Inverness 1V2 4AD
Tel: 01463 221711

BBC WALES
Broadcasting House, Llandaff, Cardiff CF5 2YQ
Tel: 01222 572888

Bangor
Broadcasting House, Meirion Road, Bangor LL57 2BY
Tel: 01248 370880

Swansea
Broadcasting House, Alexandra Road, Swansea SA1 5DZ
Tel: 01792 654986

BBC NORTHERN IRELAND
Broadcasting House, 25-27 Ormeau Avenue, Belfast BT2 8HQ
Tel: 01232 338000

INDEPENDENT TELEVISION NEWS
200-214 Gray's Inn Road, London WC1X 8XZ
Tel: 0171 833 3000

ANGLIA TELEVISION
Norwich
Anglia House, Norwich NR1 3JG
Tel: 01603 615151

Cambridge
4 Jesus Lane, Cambridge CB5 8BA
Tel: 01223 467076

Chelmsford
64-68 New London Road, Chelmsford CM2 0YU
Tel: 01245 357676

Luton
16 Park Street, Luton LU1 3EP
Tel: 01582 29666

Northampton
77B Abington Street, Northampton NN1 2BH
Tel: 01604 24343

Peterborough
28 Broadway, Peterborough PE1 1RS
Tel: 01733 346677

Ipswich
Hubbard House, Civic Drive, Ipswich IP1 2QA
Tel: 01473 226157

Milton Keynes
The Food Centre, 409 Secklow Gate East, Central Milton
Keynes MK9 3HR
Tel: 01908 691660

BORDER TELEVISION
The Television Centre, Durranhill, Carlisle CA1 3NT
Tel: 01228 25101

CARLTON TELEVISION
101 St Martin's Lane, London WC2N 4AZ
Tel: 0171 240 4000

CENTRAL TELEVISION
West Midlands
Central House, Broad Street, Birmingahm B1 2JP
Tel: 0121 643 9898

East Midlands
The Television Centre, Lenton Lane, Nottingham NG7 2NA
Tel: 01159 863322

Central South
Oxford
Unit 9, Windrush Court, Abingdon Business Park, Abingdon OX1 1SA
Tel: 01235 554123

Gloucester
Navigation House, 23-25 Commercial Road, Gloucester GL1 2ED
Tel: 01452 309666

Swindon
Hawksworth Ind. Estate, Newcombe Drive, Swindon SN2 1TV
Tel: 01793 617002

Peterborough
6 Bretton Green Village, Rightwell, Bretton, Peterborough PE3 8DY
Tel: 01733 331133

CHANNEL FOUR
124 Horseferry Road, London SW1P 2TX
Tel: 0171 396 4444

CHANNEL TELEVISION
Television Centre, La Pouquelaye, St Helier, Jersey, Channel
Islands JE2 3ZD
Tel: 01534 868999

GMTV
London Television Centre, Upper Ground, London SE1 9TT
Tel: 0171 827 7000

GRAMPIAN TELEVISION
Aberdeen
Queen's Cross, Aberdeen AB9 2XJ
Tel: 01224 646464

Dundee
Albany House, 68 Albany Road, West Ferry, Dundee DD5 1NW
Tel: 01382 739363

Inverness
23-25 Huntly Street, Inverness IV3 5PR
Tel: 01463 242624

Stornoway
Seaforth House, 54 Seaforth Road, Stornoway PA87 2SH
Tel: 01851 704433

GRANADA TELEVISION
Manchester
Granada TV Centre, Quay Street, Manchester M60 9EA
Tel: 0161 832 7211

Liverpool
Granada News Centre, Albert Dock, Liverpool L3 4AA
Tel: 0151 709 9393

Chester
Granada News Centre, Bridgegate House, 5 Bridge Place, Lower Bridge Street, Chester CH1 1SA
Tel: 01244 313966

Lancaster
Granada News Centre, White Cross, Lancaster LA1 4XQ
Tel: 01524 60688

Blackburn
Granada News Centre, Daisyfield Business Centre, Appleby Street, Blackburn BB1 3BL
Tel: 01254 690099

HTV
Cardiff
Television Centre, Culverhouse Cross, Cardiff CF5 6XJ
Tel: 01222 590590

Bristol
Television Centre, Bath Road, Bristol BS4 3HG
Tel: 01179 778366

LONDON WEEKEND TELEVISION
The Television Centre, Upper Ground, London SE1 9LT
Tel: 0171 620 1620

MERIDAN BROADCASTING
Southampton
Television Centre, Southampton SO14 OPZ
Tel: 01703 222555

Maidstone
West Point, New Hythe, Kent ME20 6XX
Tel: 01622 882244

Newbury
Brook Way, Hambridge Lane, Newbury RG14 5UZ
Tel: 01635 522322

S4C: The Welsh Fourth Channel
Parc Ty Glas, Llanishen, Cardiff CF4 5GG
Tel: 01222 747444

SCOTTISH TELEVISION
Glasgow
Cowcaddens, Glasgow G2 3PR
Tel 0141 332 9999

Edinburgh
The Gateway, Edinburgh EH7 4AH
Tel: 0131 557 4554

TYNE TEES TELEVISION
Newcastle upon Tyne
The Television Centre, City Road, Newcastle NE1 2AL
Tel: 0191 261 0181

Cleveland
Pavillion 13, Belasis Hall, Technology Park, Greenwood Road,
Billingham TS23 4AZ
Tel: 01642 566999

ULSTER TELEVISION
Havelock House, Ormeau Road, Belfast BT7 1EB
Tel: 01232 328122

WESTCOUNTRY TELEVISION
W. Wood Way, Langage Science Park, Plymouth PL7 5BG
Tel: 01752 333333

YORKSHIRE TELEVISION
Leeds
The Television Centre, Leeds LS3 1JS
Tel: 0113 2438283

Hull
23 Brook Street, The Prospect Centre, Hull HU2 8PN
Tel: 01482 24488

Sheffield
Charter Square, Sheffield S1 3EJ
Tel: 01742 723262

Lincoln
88 Bailgate, Lincoln LN1 3AR
Tel: 01522 530738

Grimsby
8 Bullring Lane, Grimsby DN31 1DY
Tel: 01472 357026

York
8 Coppergate, York YO1 1NR
Tel: 01904 610066

SATELLITE
SKY TELEVISION
6 Centaurs Business Park, Grant Way, Isleworth TW7 5QD
Tel: 0171 705 3000

NATIONAL RADIO
BBC RADIO
Broadcasting House, London W1A 1AA
Tel: 0171 580 4468

BBC RADIO SCOTLAND
Broadcasting House, Queen Margaret Drive, Glasgow G12 8DG
Tel: 0141 338 2345

Edinburgh
Broadcasting House, 5 Queen Street, Edinburgh EH2 1JF
Tel: 0131 469 4200

Aberdeen
Broadcasting House, Beechgrove Terrace, Aberdeen AB9 2ZT
Tel: 01224 625233

Inverness
Broadcasting House, 7 Culduthel Road, Inverness 1V2 4AD
Tel: 01463 720720

BBC RADIO WALES
Broadcasting House, Llandaff, Cardiff CF5 2YQ
Tel: 01222 572888

BBC RADIO NORTHERN IRELAND
Broadcasting House, 25 - 27 Ormeau Avenue, Belfast BT2 8HQ
Tel: 01232 338000

CLASSIC FM
Academic House, 24-28 Oval Road, London NW1 7DQ
Tel: 0171 284 3000

TALK RADIO UK
76 Oxford Street, London W1N OTR
Tel: 0171 636 1089

VIRGIN RADIO
1 Golden Square, London W1 3AB
Tel: 0171 434 1215

LOCAL RADIO
BBC STATIONS

RADIO ABERDEEN
Broadcasting House, Beechgrove Terrace, Aberdeen AB9 2ZT
Tel: O1224 625233

RADIO BERKSHIRE *(see Thames Valley Radio).*

RADIO BRISTOL
PO Box 194, Bristol BS99 7QT
Tel: 0117 9741111

RADIO CAMBRIDGESHIRE
104 Hills Road, Cambridge CB2 1LD
Tel: 01223 259696

RADIO CLEVELAND
Broadcasting House, PO Box 95FM, Middlesbrough TS1 5DG
Tel: 01642 225211

RADIO CORNWALL
Phoenix Wharf, Truro TR1 1UA
Tel: 01872 75421

RADIO CUMBRIA
Annetwell Street, Carlisle CA3 8BB
Tel: 01228 592444

BBC CWR
25 Warwick Road, Coventry CV1 2WR
Tel: 01203 559911

RADIO DERBY
PO Box 269 Derby DE1 3HL
Tel: 01332 361111

RADIO DEVON
PO Box 5, Broadcasting House, Seymour Road, Plymouth PL1
Tel: 01752 260323

BBC ESSEX
198 New London Road, Chelmsford CM2 9XB
Tel: 01245 262393

RADIO GLOUCESTERSHIRE
London Road, Gloucester GL1 1SW
Tel: 01452 308585

BBC GLR
PO Box 94.9 35c Marylebone High Street, London W1A 4LG
Tel: 0171 224 2424

BBC GMR
New Broadcasting House, PO Box 951, Oxford Road,
Manchester M60 1SD
Tel: 0161 200 2000

RADIO GUERNSEY
Commerce House, Les Banques, St Peter Port, Guernsey GY1
2HS
Tel: 01481 728977

BBC HEREFORD & WORCESTER
Hylton Road, Worcester WR2 5WW
Tel: 01905 748485

RADIO HUMBERSIDE
9 Chapel Street, Hull HU1 3NU
Tel: 01482 323232

RADIO JERSEY
18 Parade Road, St Helier, Jersey JE2 3PL
Tel: 01534 870000

RADIO KENT
Sun Pier, Chatham ME4 4EZ
Tel: 01634 830505

RADIO LANCASHIRE
Darwen Street, Blackburn BB2 2EA
Tel: 01254 262411

RADIO LEEDS
Broadcasting House, Woodhouse Lane, Leeds LS2 9PN
Tel: 0113 2442131

RADIO LEICESTER
Epic House, Charles Street, Leicester LE1 3SH
Tel: 0116 2516688

RADIO LINCOLNSHIRE
PO Box 219, Newport, Lincoln LN1 3XY
Tel: 01522 511411

RADIO MERSEYSIDE
55 Paradise Street, Liverpool L1 3BP
Tel: 0151 708 5500

RADIO NEWCASTLE
Broadcasting Centre, Newcastle upon Tyne NE99 1RN
Tel: 0191 232 4141

RADIO NORFOLK
Norfolk Tower, Surrey Street, Norwich NR1 3PA
Tel: 01603 617411

RADIO NORTHAMPTON
Broadcasting House, Abington Street, Northampton NN1 2BH
Tel: 01604 239100

RADIO NOTTINGHAM
PO Box 222 Nottingham NG1 3HZ
Tel: 0115 9550500

RADIO OXFORD (see Thames Valley Radio).

RADIO PETERBOROUGH
PO Box 957, Peterborough PE1 1YT
Tel: 01733 312832

RADIO SHEFFIELD
60 Westbourne Road, Sheffield S10 2QU
Tel: 0114 2686185

RADIO SHROPSHIRE
2-4 Boscobel Drive, Shrewsbury SY1 3TT
Tel: 01743 248484

RADIO SOLENT
Broadcasting House, Havelock Road, Southampton SO1 0XR
Tel: 01703 631311

BBC SOMERSET SOUND
14-15 Paul Street, Taunton TA1 3PF
Tel: 01823 252437

BBC SOUTHERN COUNTIES RADIO
Broadcasting Centre, Guildford GU2 5AP
Tel: 01483 306306

RADIO STOKE
Cheapside, Hanley, Stoke On Trent ST1 1JJ
Tel: 01782 208080

RADIO SUFFOLK
Broadcasting House, St Matthews Street, Ipswich IP1 3EP
Tel: 01473 250000

THAMES VALLEY RADIO
269, Banbury Road, Oxford OX2 7DW
Tel: 01865 311444 *(Launched Spring 1996 following the merger of Radio Oxford and Radio Berkshire).*

BBC THREE COUNTIES RADIO
PO Box 3CR, Hastings Street, Luton LU1 5XL
Tel: 01582 441000

BBC WILTSHIRE SOUND
Broadcasting House, Prospect Place, Swindon SN1 3RW
Tel: 01793 513626

BBC RADIO WM/WCR
PO Box 206, Birmingham B5 7SD
Tel: 0121 414 8484

RADIO YORK
20 Bootham Row, York YO3 7BR
Tel: 01904 641351

SCOTLAND
RADIO HIGHLAND
Broadcasting House, 7 Culduthel Road, Inverness IV2 4AD
Tel: 01463 720720

RADIO ORKNEY
Castle Street, Kirkwall KW15 1DF
Tel: 01856 873939

RADIO SCOTLAND (BORDERS)
Municipal Buildings, High Street, Selkirk TD7 4BU
Tel: 01750 21884

RADIO SCOTLAND (DUMFRIES)
Elmbank, Lover's Walk, Dumfries DG1 1NZ
Tel: 01387 268008

RADIO SHETLAND
Brentham House, Lerwick ZE1 0LR
Tel: 01595 694747

WALES
BBC RADIO WALES IN CLWYD
The Old School House, Glanrafon Road, Mold CH7 1PA
Tel: 01352 700367

IRELAND
RADIO FOYLE
8 Northland Road, Londonderry BT 48 7JT
Tel: 01504 262244

RADIO ULSTER
Broadcasting House, Ormeau Avenue, Belfast BT2 8HQ
Tel: 01232 338000

INDEPENDENT STATIONS
AIRE FM/ MAGIC 828
PO Box 2000, 51 Burley Road, Leeds LS3 1LR
Tel: 0113 2452299

BEACON RADIO/ WABC
267 Tettenhall Road, Wolverhampton WV6 0DQ
Tel: 01902 757211

96.4 FM BRMB FM/XTRA AM
Radio House, Aston Road North, Birmingham B6 4BX
Tel: 0121 359 4481

BROADLAND 102
St Georges Plain, 47-49 Colegate, Norwich NR3 1DB
Tel: 01603 630621

CAPITAL FM/ CAPITAL GOLD
Euston Tower, London NW1 3DR
Tel: 0171 608 6080

CENTURY RADIO
Century House, PO Box 100, Church Street, Gateshead NE8 2YY
Tel: 0191 477 6666

CFM
PO Box 964, Carlisle CA1 3NG
Tel: 01228 818964

CHILTERN RADIO
Chiltern Road, Dunstable LU6 1HQ
Tel: 01582 666001

RADIO CITY/ CITY FM/ RADIO CITY GOLD
PO Box 194, 8-10 Stanley Street, Liverpool L1 6AF
Tel: 0151 227 5100

RADIO CLYDE/ CLYDE 1 FM/ CLYDE 2
Clydebank Business Park, Clydebank G81 2RX
Tel: 0141 306 2272

ESSEX FM/BREEZE
Radio House, Clifftown Road, Southend on Sea SS1 1SX
Tel: 01702 333711

FORTUNE 1458
PO Box 1458, Quay West, Trafford Park, Manchester M17 1FL
Tel: 0161 872 1458

FOX FM
Brush House, Pony Road, Cowley, Oxford OX4 2XR
Tel: 01865 748787

GEM-AM
29-31 Castle Gate, Nottingham NG1 7AP
Tel: 0115 9581731

GEMINI RADIO FM/AM
Hawthorn House, Exeter Business Park, Exeter EX1 3QS
Tel: 01392 444444

GWR FM (WEST)/ BRUNEL CLASSIC GOLD
PO Box 2000 (Brunel: PO Box 2020) Bristol BS99 7SN
Tel: 0117 9843200

HALLAM FM
Radio House, 900 Herries Road, Sheffield S6 1RH
Tel: 0114 2853333

HEART FM
1 The Square, 111 Broad Street, Birmingham B15 1AS
Tel: 0121 626 1007

HEREWARD FM
PO Box 225, Queensgate Centre, Peterborough PE1 1XJ
Tel: 01733 460460

HORIZON RADIO
Broadcast Centre, Crownhill, Milton Keynes MK8 0AB
Tel: 01908 269111

INVICTA FM/ INVICTA SUPERGOLD
PO Box 100, Whitstable CT5 3QX
Tel: 01227 772004

ISLE OF WIGHT RADIO
Dodnor Park, Newport
Tel: 01983 822557

LEICESTER SOUND FM
Granville House, Granville Road, Leicester LE1 7RW
Tel: 0116 2561300

LONDON NEWS 97.3 FM/ LONDON NEWS TALK 1152 AM
72 Hammersmith Road, London W14 8YE
Tel: 0171 973 1152

MERCIA FM/ MERCIA CLASSIC GOLD
Mercia Sound Ltd, Hertford Place, Coventry CV1 3TT
Tel: 01203 868200

MERCURY FM/ MERCURY EXTRA AM
Broadfield House, Brighton Road, Crawley RH11 9TT
Tel: 01293 519161

METRO FM/ GREAT NORTH RADIO
Swalwell, Newcastle upon Tyne NE99 1BB
Tel: 0191 488 3131/ 496 0337

OCEAN FM/ SOUTH COAST RADIO
Whittle Avenue, Segensworth West, Fareham PO15 5PA
Tel: 01489 589911

ORCHARD FM
Haygrove House, Shoreditch, Taunton TA3 7BT
Tel: 01823 338448

PICCADILLY GOLD/ KEY 103
127-131 The Piazza, Piccadilly Plaza, Manchester M1 4AW
Tel: 0161 236 9913

PLYMOUTH SOUND FM/AM
Earl's Acre, Alma Road, Plymouth PL3 4HX
Tel: 01752 227272

THE PULSE/ GREAT YORKSHIRE GOLD
Forster Square, Bradford BD1 5NE
Tel: 01274 731521
Also at: Great Yorkshire Gold, PO Box 777, Sheffield S6 1RH
Tel: 0114 853333

Q103 FM
PO Box 103, Vision Park, Chivers Way, Histon, Cambridge CB4
Tel: 01223 235255

RED ROSE GOLD/ ROCK FM
PO Box 301, St Paul's Square, Preston PR1 1YE
Tel: 01772 556301

SEVERN SOUND/ SEVERN SOUND SUPERGOLD
67 Southgate Street, Gloucester GL1 2DQ
Tel: 01452 423791

SGR FM 97.1/96.4
Alpha Business Park, Whitehouse Road, Ipswich IP1 5LT
Tel: 01473 461000

SIGNAL CHESHIRE
Regent House, Heaton Lane, Stockport SK4 1BX
Tel: 0161 480 5445

SIGNAL ONE/ SIGNAL GOLD/ SIGNAL STAFFORD
Studio 257, Stoke Road, Stoke on Trent ST4 2SR
Tel: 01782 747047

SOUTHERN FM
PO Box 2000, Brighton BN41 2SS
Tel: 01273 430111

SPECTRUM RADIO
Endeavour House, Brent Cross, London NW2 1JT
Tel: 0181 905 5000

SPIRE FM
City Hall Studios, Malthouse Lane, Salisbury SP2 7QQ
Tel: 01722 416644

TRENT FM
29-31 Castlegate, Nottingham NG1 7AP
Tel: 0115 9581731

2CR (TWO COUNTIES RADIO)
5-7 Southcote Road, Bournemouth BH1 3LR
Tel: 01202 294881

2-TEN FM/ CLASSIC GOLD 1431
PO Box 210, Reading RG3 5RZ
Tel: 01734 254400

VIKING FM
Commercial Road, Hull HU1 2SA
Tel: 01482 325141

WEAR FM, 103.4
Foster Building, Chester Road, Sunderland SR1 3SD
Tel: 0191 515 2103

WESSEX FM
Radio House, Trinity Street, Dorchester DT1 1DJ
Tel: 01305 250333

1332 WGMS
PO Box 225, Queensgate Centre, Peterborough PE1 1XJ
Tel: 01733 460460

RADIO WYVERN
PO Box 22, 5-6 Barbourne Terrace, Worcester WR1 3JZ
Tel: 01905 612212

SCOTLAND
RADIO BORDERS
Tweedside Park, Tweedbank, Galashiels TD1 3TD
Tel: 01896 759444

FORTH FM/ MAX AM
Forth House, Forth Street, Edinburgh EH1 3LF
Tel: 0131 556 9255

MORAY FIRTH RADIO
PO Box 271, Scorgvie Place, Inverness IV3 6SF
Tel: 01463 224433

NORTHSOUND RADIO
45 King's Gate, Aberdeen AB2 6BL
Tel: 01224 632234

SCOT FM
Number 1 Shed, Albert Quay, Leith, Edinburgh EH6 7DN
Tel: 0131 554 6677 *Also at: Anderston Quay, Glasgow G3 8DA*
Tel: 0141 204 1003

RADIO TAY
PO Box 123, Dundee DD1 9UF
Tel: 01382 200800

WEST SOUND RADIO/ SOUTH WEST SOUND FM
Radio House, 54 Holmston Road, Ayr KA7 3BE
Tel: 01292 283662

WALES
MARCHER SOUND
The Studios, Mold Road, Wrexham LL11 4AF
Tel: 01978 752202

RED DRAGON FM/ TOUCH AM
Radio House, West Canal Wharf, Cardiff CF1 5XJ
Tel: 01222 384041/ 237878

SWANSEA SOUND
Victoria Road, Gowerton, Swansea SA4 3AB
Tel: 01792 893751

IRELAND
DOWNTOWN RADIO/ COOL FM
Newtownards, Co. Down BT23 4ES
Tel: 01247 815555

NEWS AGENCIES
ASSOCIATED PRESS
12 Norwich Street, London EC4A 1BP
Tel: 0171 353 1515/ 353 6323

NATIONAL NEWS AGENCY
30 St John's Lane, London EC1M 4BJ
Tel: 0171 417 7707

PRESS ASSOCATION
292 Vauxhall Bridge Road, London SW1V 1AE
Tel: 0171 963 7000

REUTERS LTD
85 Fleet Street, London EC4P 4AJ
Tel: 0171 250 1122

MORE FROM OTTER PUBLICATIONS.......

WHEELS OF JUSTICE (1 899053 02 6, £5.95, 128 pp) by *Duncan Callow*, is aimed at all, including the legal profession, who would like to find out more about how they would stand legally in any given motoring situation. The easy to understand style makes it extremely accessible and contains a useful glossary of terms to clearly spell out all the legal jargon used. *WHEELS OF JUSTICE* is intended as a practical handbook and draws upon many of the author's experiences, both professional and personal. Key areas covered include:

- Insurance
- The MOT and vehicle safety
- Accidents and dealing with their aftermath
- Drink driving and related offences
- The major motoring offences
- The court process
- The fixed penalty system and the penalty points system
- Parking offences and wheel clamping
- Basic motorcycle law
- Driving on the continent
- Buying a used car

"This highly readable law book covers all aspects of driving...useful facts abound". AutoExpress.

"The driver's bible". The News of the World.

"I doubt whether you will find a better introduction to the subject....I recommend it most highly". Learner Driver.

BEHIND THE WHEEL: the learner driver's handbook (1 899053 04 2, 264 pp, £7.95), also by *Graham Yuill*, is a step-by-step, highly illustrated handbook. Now into its fourth edition, the book **features a full colour section and questions and answers to help the learner driver learn to drive and pass the theory driving test.** *BEHIND THE WHEEL* will teach the reader all aspects of driving and road safety in 20 easy lessons The teaching methods used are those laid down by The Driving Standards Agency. A completely up-to-date section on trams has also been included. Finally the events of the driving test day are outlined in full with useful advice and tips.

"Anyone who is learning to drive, or teaching someone else, will **appreciate Behind the Wheel".** *Woman and Home.*

BUYING YOUR NEXT CAR: your questions answered (1 899053 07 7, 96 pp, £3.95) is packed with essential information which will help all would-be car buyers of second-hand cars make the right decision. Given that buying a car is the second most expensive purchase that an individual will make, it is vital to get it right. This book contains over one hundred questions. *DON'T BUY A USED CAR UNTIL YOU HAVE READ THIS BOOK - IT MAY WELL SAVE YOU POUNDS!* The key areas covered include:

- How to choose your car
- Finding a genuine used car
- The structural and mechanical assessment
- The test drive
- Used cars and the law
- Coping with dealers and sellers
- Motor vehicle auctions
- Looking after your 'new' car

ADVERTISING FOR THE SMALL BUSINESS: how to reach maximum sales for minimum cost (1 899053 08 5, 160 pp, £7.95). Sales are the lifeblood of any business. If you are self-employed, running a small business or handling the marketing for a small company, then this book is for you. *ADVERTISING FOR THE SMALL BUSINESS* is a practical guide and provides an introduction to advertising for small businesses where budgets may be limited but sales vital in an increasingly competitive environment. The book explains about:

- The purpose of advertising
- Classified advertisements
- Display advertising
- Other forms of advertising
- Sales letters
- Direct response
- Sales promotions and point-of-sale advertising
- Public relations

How to order:-

Through your local bookshop or in case of difficulty, please send a cheque made payable to Grantham Book Services Ltd., Isaac Newton Way, Alma Park Ind. Estate, Grantham, Lincolnshire, NG31 9SD. Tel: 01476 67421, Fax: 01476 67314 or your credit card details.